The Story of the Penny Black
and its Contemporaries

Front of the *Post Magazine,* issue number 2, a privately printed weekly letter sheet, used from London to Melrose on 12th August 1840.

The whole document was sold for one penny complete with an unused One Penny stamp: the publishers made a profit on the advertising it carried.

National Postal Museum, London.

The Story of the Penny Black
and its Contemporaries

A. G. Rigo de Righi
BA FRPS,L

Curator
The National Postal Museum
London

The National Postal Museum
London

First published 1980

The National Postal Museum
King Edward Building
King Edward Street
London EC1A 1LP

Designed by Frank Overton FSIAD FSTD

Printed at The House of Questa
London England

ISBN 0 9500018 7 2

Contents

Dedication

To the late Reginald M. Phillips CBE,
a dedicated student of the Penny Black,
whose munificent gift of his collection
to the Nation furnished the inspiration
for this book.

A. G. R. de R.

The introduction of Uniform (Penny) Postage in Great Britain on 10th January 1840 is one of the great landmarks in the history of communications. It was, largely, the work of Rowland Hill whose imaginative and practical reform had, in the words of the great Liberal Statesman, Mr. Gladstone, *'run like wildfire through the civilised world: never perhaps was a local invention and improvement applied in the lifetime of its author to the advantages of such vast multitudes of his fellow-creatures.'*

Familiar as one is today with the essential part of Hill's revolutionary new postal system – the operation of a uniform scale of prepaid postal charges assessed by weight only and irrespective of distance – it is not, at first glance, easy to appreciate fully the enormous economic and social impact made by his great reform of 1840. But it had within his lifetime a beneficial effect on communications worldwide; in less than 40 years his system had been adopted by some 150 territories throughout the world.

One essential part of the new system was the creation of convenient methods of prepayment of postage on letters. These consisted of special prepaid stationery (envelopes and letter sheets) and, most significant of all, adhesive labels which paid in advance the appropriate postal charges to take the letters on to which they had been stuck to their various destinations. These labels became known as postage stamps.

This book is concerned with the story of the invention and production of the world's first adhesive postage stamps and the contemporary stamped stationery, followed by an account of why and how they had to be replaced by other stamps and envelopes after only 9 months. But there was no change whatsoever in the idea of prepaying postage by means of a gummed printed label, which had proved most popular and a resounding success; while the design used for the Penny Black seems to have been so satisfactory that, with only minor changes, it continued in use for exactly 40 years and was imitated in its essentials by many foreign countries.

Every postal administration in the world now uses postage stamps for the prepayment of mail – by the end of 1978, some 200,000 different stamps had been issued in all shapes and sizes and 'printed' by a dozen different processes ranging from typewriting to multi-colour photogravure.

But the first postage stamp, the One Penny Black of May 1840, remains pre-eminent, not only as the very first stamp but also as an exceptional example of miniature design, engraving and printing.

'Is this the General Post, Sir?'

'Yes, Mum.'

'Then will you just have the goodness to stamp upon my little boy here, and send him off to Gravesend!'

An amusing cartoon by John Leech suggesting the possibilities of the benefits of penny postage.

The Postal System before 1839-40

Nearly 350 years ago, on 31st July 1635, King Charles I issued a proclamation from his Court at Bagshot establishing the first state postal service for the conveyance of private letters within England and Scotland, and appointing a certain Thomas Witherings to organise it. Previously, there had been only a King's or Queen's Post, used principally for the swift carriage of Royal and State correspondence; the first Master of the Posts Sir Brian Tuke having been appointed by King Henry VIII in 1510.

From 1635, in return for fixed rates of postage whose proceeds went to the Crown, there was to operate a new framework of regular post routes for England and Scotland. There was already a service for letters to and from 'Foreign Parts.' The new inland postage rates were based on distance (varying from 2d for under 80 miles to 8d for carriage to the Scottish border and beyond for a 'single' letter of one sheet) and the number of sheets. Since the value of the 1635 penny was considerable, the new State post, though convenient, was far from cheap. Moreover the new post was a Crown monopoly and power was given to suppress all forms of competition in the carrying of letters by such persons as itinerant chapman (peddlers) or the common carriers who took goods by cart or packhorse between towns and villages.

During the two centuries which followed up to 1839 there were naturally many changes in the postal system.

In 1660, a Royal Proclamation established the General Post Office to succeed the Posts of Witherings and the Cromwellian Protectorate in the carriage of private letters between towns in England and Scotland and also to places overseas. Henry Bishop, Postmaster General (PMG) 1660-1663 introduced the first British handstamps on letters in 1661 and in 1680 William Dockwra and some fellow merchants started a private local service for London, the first such in the world. Dockwra's venture – a Penny Post – was so successful that it was taken over by the Crown in 1682 as the London and District Post, and the rate continued at 1d per letter.

During the eighteenth century Cross Posts (directly between large towns instead of being routed through London) and Mail Coach services (using the rapidly improving road network) were started by Ralph Allen and John Palmer respectively.

In 1801 the London Penny Post became a Two-penny Post to help finance the long war against Napoleon. At about the same time local Penny Posts were being established to serve areas round existing Post Offices in the towns, but their charges were in addition to those of the General Post. From 1830 onwards mails were further accelerated by being transferred from the coaches to the new railways.

Though the various changes led to a great improvement in the speed of mails and a wide extension of the postal network, over the years the way the postal system operated became ever more complicated and so more difficult and more expensive to work.

The Need for Postal Reform

The principal function of the Post Office in 1837, the year of Queen Victoria's accession, was what it had been since Stuart times, the production of the greatest possible revenue for the Crown. Some of the money was given to Royal favourites and even as late as 1855 the descendents of one of Charles II's mistresses, the Duchess of Cleveland, still benefited from Post Office surpluses. By 1812 postal charges had gradually been increased to 4d for up to 15 miles and 8d up to 80 miles (for a single letter). These charges, which were mostly collected on delivery rather than by prepayment, were not based on costs but on the requirements of the Treasury [illustration 1].

1 Postman at a house door to deliver, and collect postage on unpaid letters. *Print c.1810.*

Such excessive (and unjustified) postal charges inevitably led not only to agitation for reform but also to evasion. Members of both Houses of Parliament, amongst others, were entitled to free postage (franking). Banks and commercial companies elected Peers and MPs to their boards of directors to obtain the benefit of their franks. Illegal posts functioned between main towns, while the recipients of letters on which high postage was due, often refused to accept them once they had recognised the handwriting of the sender and were therefore assured that he or she was alive and well.

It is not surprising that Post Office net revenue was stagnant, even actually in decline, and this in spite of a steady increase in the population.

By 1837 it was becoming very clear that high postal charges, by throttling written communication, were seriously affecting the spread of learning and literacy and even more the expansion of trade and manufacture. People were moving in large numbers from the countryside into the new industrial centres and they quickly lost touch with relatives and friends. At a time when many workmen earned no more than 6s6d or 7s6d per week the cost of sending letters (on average 8½d) discouraged any wish to learn how to read or write them. And industry, if it were to grow and prosper, required an increasingly educated, and therefore literate, labour force.

Even more important the expansion of both industry and trade depended more and more on cheap means of written communications; invoices, bills, price lists, receipts, commercial enquiries and the rest, all costing at least 4d each to send by post (except within London) at a time when 4d was equivalent to some £2 in present-day money.

2 (Sir) Rowland Hill, about 1835. *Lithograph of a drawing by W. Taylor.*

Rowland Hill's Proposals for Post Office Reform

From 1830 onwards mounting criticism of this situation was being voiced by influential men, such as Charles Knight, a publisher who became the Superintendent of the Society for the Diffusion of Useful Knowledge. Knight had worked hard to promote education and learning amongst the labouring classes but found his work frustrated by the fact that though newspapers and magazines paid no postage (and therefore helped keep postage on letters high) they had to pay a newspaper tax as well as being printed on paper which was also taxed. In 1834 he suggested collecting prepaid postage on newspapers by means of stamped wrappers at one penny each (while the newspaper and paper taxes were to be abolished).
There were many other critics including Robert Wallace, the first MP for Greenock, a new constituency created by the Reform Bill (it was an age of reform), James Chalmers (a Dundee bookseller, of whom more later) and Charles Babbage the inventor.

As a result of this pressure Special Commissioners appointed to enquire into the management of various departments of the Post Office issued between 1835 and 1837 no less than 9 reports which, though they made no significant proposals for change, did provide the necessary facts and figures on which any plans for reform must depend.

In January 1837 however a former schoolmaster named Rowland Hill produced a privately-printed pamphlet entitled *'Post Office Reform – its Importance and Practicability'* which not only used the Commissioner's reports to analyse the shortcomings of the existing postal system but also spelt out detailed and highly-practical plans for reform. Rowland Hill then aged 41 [illus. 2], was a notable example of the way Britain in the nineteenth century produced men and women of vision and talent, who proved to be outstanding in each enterprise they undertook. Hill, for instance, was already well known as an educational reformer, an advocate of social communities, an inventor in the fields of printing, screw propulsion and road-making and, since 1835, as the Secretary to the South Australian Colonization Commission.

An important part of Hill's critical examination (in his lengthy pamphlet) of the existing postal system was an analysis of the actual cost of conveyance and handling of mail over specific routes. He was able to show, for instance, that the £5 which the Post Office normally spent in sending each day's mail from London to Edinburgh, worked out at an average of just over one-third of a penny per letter, whereas the amount of postage per letter actually charged was 1s1½d! Moreover the cost of conveyance per letter would have been greatly less had not the bulk of each mail consisted of (free) newspapers and postfree privilege letters from MPs and officials [illus. 3].

3 Cartoon by Henry Cole to illustrate the disproportionate weight of 'Free' and 'Paid' mail carried on the London-Edinburgh mail coaches. *From the Post Circular.*

More generally, Rowland Hill pin-pointed the high costs of letter distribution (which led to high postage rates) as being for the most part the result of over-complex arrangements at the Post Office. Such complex arrangements, he wrote, could be avoided if postage were charged at a uniform rate, *according to weight and without any regard to distance* or to the number of sheets, and if it were collected in advance. Moreover, he claimed, it would be practicable to collect postage in advance if it were reduced to the flat rate he proposed: one penny for each letter or packet not exceeding ½oz in weight; each additional ½oz to be charged an additional penny.

Finally he also suggested alternative methods for prepayment: in cash at the Post Office counter (this was already possible), by the purchase of prepaid

Government-stamped stationery, and by the official stamping of private letter sheets or envelopes. But the additional method he suggested on 13th February 1837, in giving evidence to The Commission of Post Office Enquiry, proved to be really dramatic – though Hill himself only produced it as an after-thought. In cases, he said, where an illiterate or dishonest servant were sent to a Post Office with a letter not written on or enclosed inside officially stamped stationery, *'This difficulty might be obviated by using a bit of paper just large enough to bear the "stamp" and covered at the back with a glutinous wash which the bringer might, by applying a little moisture attach to the......letter.....'*

Rowland Hill's pamphlet caused an immediate sensation and there were two further editions within a short space of time. The conclusions and proposals for reform, though they met with considerable criticism from some quarters including the officials of the Post Office, were exactly what the merchants, the educationalists and many others were looking for and a powerful movement for speedy postal reform developed almost overnight.

The crucial action came from Robert Wallace, the Greenock MP. In December 1837 he successfully proposed that the House of Commons should set up a Committee to examine Hill's proposals, and he became its Chairman. After taking evidence, and in spite of strong opposition, the Committee (on Wallace's casting vote as Chairman) reported in favour of the plan.

Meantime, outside Parliament, vigorous propaganda in support of the plan was being carried on by the Mercantile Committee, a group of influential City of London businessmen under the guidance of Henry Cole who had recently made a reputation by re-organising the Public Record Office and was soon to become Hill's invaluable assistant at the Treasury. The Mercantile Committee organised numerous petitions to Parliament, worked up enthusiasm for the plan in the industrial centres (largely through Mechanics Institutes) and, perhaps most effective of all, published its own propaganda news sheet *The Post Circular* which, as a registered (taxed) newspaper, was sent free through the post.

In August 1839, virtually all Rowland Hill's proposals for uniform, prepaid, penny postage were embodied in a new Act of Parliament. Because provisions of the Act involved revenue, it was left to the Treasury, not the Post Office, to carry them into effect.

During the long struggle, within Parliament and outside it, to give effect by the force of law to Hill's proposals, both the Postmaster General, Lord Lichfield, and the Secretary to the Post Office, Colonel Maberley, had denounced Hill's ideas in the strongest terms. Maberley described the plan as *'most preposterous'* and *'utterly unsupported by the facts'* while Lichfield declared that *'of all the wild and visionary schemes I have ever heard or read of, it is the most extraordinary.'* But he had later been forced, in Parliament, to withdraw his active opposition *'on the simple ground that the demand for the measure was universal.'*

It was generally assumed that Rowland Hill as the author of the plan would be asked to assist in its execution. It was no surprise therefore that on 16th September 1839 Hill was appointed to a very senior (but vaguely defined) post at the Treasury. In view of Maberley's continued hostility, Mr. Francis Baring the Liberal Chancellor of the Exchequer was able to reassure Hill that *'you will find from myself and the Board (of the Treasury) that confidence and cordiality which will be necessary for the well-working of the proposed alterations.'* Francis Baring was as good as his word; he gave Hill all necessary support in the latter's frequent differences with Maberley and a virtually free hand in directing the selection, design and production of the various kinds of 'stamps' which were necessary to the carrying out of the new Penny Post system.

Earliest Ideas for 'Stamps'

Ten days before Hill's appointment, the Lords of the Treasury issued a notice, carried in *The Times* and other newspapers, advertising a competition open to artists, scientists and the general public in connection with the forthcoming introduction of prepaid postage and a Uniform Penny Post. The published rules asked for ideas, in the widest sense, for stamped covers and adhesive postage labels, for the security of such items against forgery and the convenience of their use, from both the public and postal servants. To stimulate interest, awards of £200 and £100 were offered for the two best suggestions.

The response was overwhelming and typical of the energy and talent of the Victorians. Suggestions poured into the Treasury by every post: on 21st September Hill recorded in his diary that *'about 30 letters a day are now received at the Treasury on the subject of Penny Postage.'* There were even several from France and Belgium – until finally over 2,600 suggestions, designs and samples had been submitted by 15th October, the closing date.

Although the Treasury Board on 2nd December actually awarded four £100 prizes (instead of two), Rowland Hill had decided (and convinced Baring) that none of the entries were, in themselves, completely suitable though several incorporated useful ideas. Nevertheless the sketches and sample designs produced by the prizewinners and many of the other entries are of great interest and importance as virtually the world's first trials ('essays') for adhesive postage stamps and for prepaid postal stationery.

James Chalmers' Essays

To James Chalmers, the Dundee bookseller, must go the honour of having produced the world's very first trial postage stamps ('essays'). These were a strip of five square labels, printed letterpress in pale red with fancy borders, and attached to a letter which Chalmers wrote to the Post Office on 10th February 1838, now in the R. M. Phillips Collection at the National Postal Museum (NPM). Chalmers also submitted two entries for the Treasury Competition (on 30th September and 7th October 1839). These later postage labels (1d and 2d values) were circular and somewhat larger, printed some in black and some in red. They were stuck on to dummy letters and cancelled, as Chalmers proposed, with a handstamp giving the town name (Dundee) and the date [illus. 4]. In his letter to Rowland Hill accompanying the 1839 essays Chalmers wrote *'If slips or stamps are to be used I flatter myself that I have a claim to priority – it now being nearly two years since I first made it public......'* Chalmer's claim to have been the first to have *proposed* the idea, was, unfortunately for him, incorrect. In January 1840 Rowland Hill wrote to Chalmers pointing out that he (Hill) had suggested adhesive labels or stamps in his 1837 pamphlet and this claim was virtually admitted by Chalmers himself four months later.

James Chalmers died in 1853 but his claim was revived by his son Patrick and passionately upheld in many books and articles, the first being published very shortly after Sir Rowland Hill's death in 1879. The controversy has been continued by members of both families right up to the present day.

The answer is surely that each of the two men concerned, Hill and Chalmers, contributed to the birth of the adhesive postage stamp. The credit for the idea

4 Treasury Competition essay by James Chalmers dated, *in manuscript*, 1st October 1839. *National Postal Museum, London.*

must certainly go to Rowland Hill who certainly adapted it from the adhesive stamps which had been used for the payment of various fiscal duties for well over a century before February 1837.

To James Chalmers belongs the honour of being the first man to give the idea form, in the shape of the rather crude labels ('essays') which he designed and produced in 1838 and again in September 1839. He should also be credited with the idea of using the town name and date to cancel the new postage stamp – a practice now almost universal but not generally adopted throughout Britain until the end of the century.

But equally Chalmers had little or no idea of the practical problems – security, cost and speed of printing allied to fine design – involved in the production of effective adhesive postage stamps. These problems Rowland Hill determined and solved with skill and taste and he is therefore rightly honoured as the Father of the Postage Stamp.

Treasury Competition Ideas

A substantial proportion, perhaps as much as a quarter, of the 2,600 entries for the Treasury Competition have survived, the majority of them in the collection of H.M. The Queen and in the R. M. Phillips and Post Office collection in the National Postal Museum.

These designs and essays can be roughly divided into those for stamped envelopes or letter sheets on the one hand (the great majority) and a much smaller group (less than 50) which are ideas for adhesive labels or 'stamped' letter seals. The great variety and inventiveness in the ideas submitted by these very early Victorians is truly remarkable. But if one examines representative examples of both envelopes and 'labels' one begins to see why none of them were wholly suited to the purpose for which they were intended.

Taking the envelopes first, one finds that several competitors submitted hand-drawn designs, notably the anonymous designer of a group of 11 envelopes, one of which is illustrated overleaf [illus. 5]. These bore various heraldic devices (such as the arms of London, Ireland, Scotland etc) on the left and an inscription stating the postage rate or area for which they were valid e.g. 'General Ireland envelope.'

5 One of a set of eleven Treasury Competition essays by an unknown competitor. *NPM.*

Attractive though these are, it is difficult to see them as practical for general use in the Letter Post.

With the printed designs, we enter the realm of the practical, but many of the simpler printed envelopes would have been too open to forgery to be adopted by the Treasury. But no one could complain that the designs and essays submitted by other competitors such as John Dickinson lacked complexity. Dickinson was a paper manufacturer and both his envelopes were printed on his own patented silk-thread paper [illus. 6 opposite]. Perhaps the most interesting envelope essay was that submitted by James Wyld who held the appointment of Geographer to the Queen [illus. 7 opposite]. The design with its allegorical figures and floral garlands is far more artistic than the geometrical patterns favoured by most other competitors and therefore nearer to Rowland Hill's own ideas.

Other Essays for Postage Stamp Labels

As with the envelopes, the stamp label essays submitted for the Treasury Competition fall into several distinct groups, each one incorporating important ideas which have influenced the design and production of adhesive postage stamps from 1840 onwards. None however were suitable in themselves, for one reason or another.

8 Lithographed multi-colour essay for a 'label' submitted for the Treasury Competition by Myers & Co. of London. *NPM.*

9 Multi-coloured engraved essays for 'labels' submitted for the Treasury Competition by Charles Whiting. *NPM.*

Myers and Co. and Charles Whiting (both of London) produced essays [illus. 8 and 9] which were specially designed to be proof against forgery. They used several

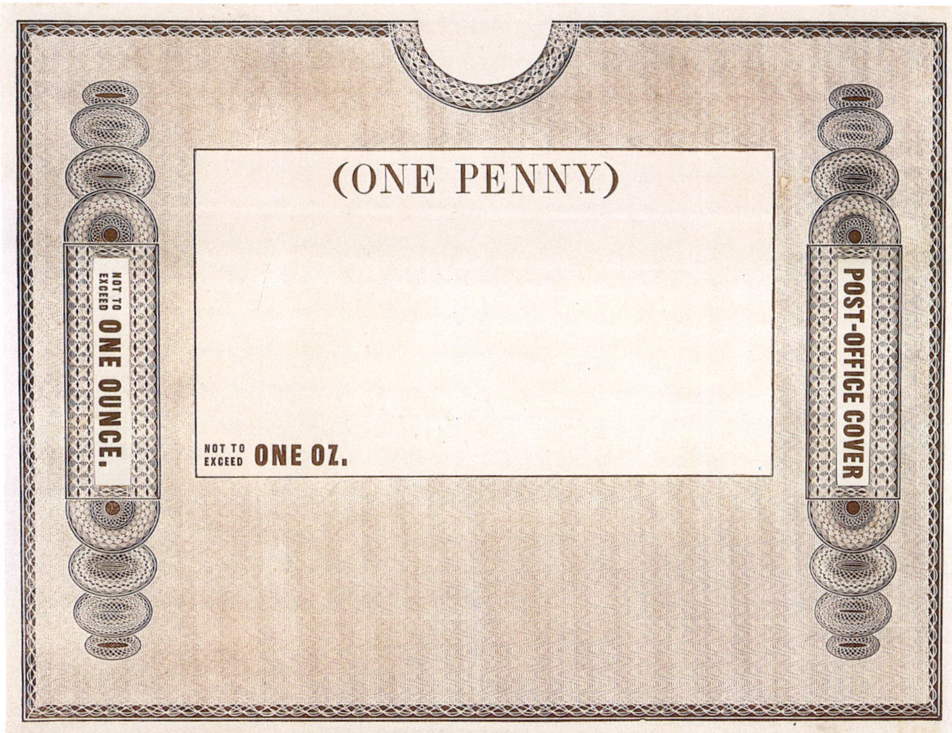

6 Treasury Competition essay for a letter sheet submitted by John Dickinson. *NPM.*

7 Treasury Competition essay for an envelope submitted by James Wyld, geographer to the Queen. *NPM.*

10 Eight hand-drawn essays for 'labels' submitted for the Treasury Competition by George Dickinson. *NPM.*

printing processes – letterpress, lithography, embossing, engraving etc. – either singly or combined as well as several colours and extremely elaborate geometrical designs. Some were also printed on watermarked papers. Unfortunately their very complexity made them both slow and expensive to produce and thus impractical.

George Dickinson and a Mr. Pewtress of London both hit on the idea of producing several labels of different face value to meet the various new postage rates. Those by Dickinson, which are hand-drawn in ink [illus. 10], also specify the particular postage rate for which each of the labels, in differing designs, was intended – the 1/- value for instance, was inscribed 'AMERICAN LETTER.'

Finally we come to the very distinctive essay by William Wyon RA, the Chief Engraver to the Royal Mint, who had created the fine head of the young Queen Victoria on the medal struck to commemorate her Coronation visit to the City of London [illus. 11]. This medal head was to become the original of many representations of the Queen on the British and Colonial postage stamps issued throughout her long reign. Wyon's essay [see illus. 12 on page 15] is of particular interest because it is almost the only Treasury Competition design to use the sovereign's head as the central motif of a stamp. It is hand-drawn in ink, but though it is nearer to the issued stamp than any other submitted, it somehow failed to win Wyon an award.

In general most of the entries for the competition were quite unsuitable. But Rowland Hill *was* able to make use – though in a considerably modified form – of a few of the ideas put forward to produce acceptable stamps and stationery. These certainly included the use of watermarked paper; the use of the sovereign's head as the central part of the design, suggested by both Wyon and Cheverton (who was one of the prizewinners); the use of an elaborate security background; and possibly the security against forgery given by the use of embossing or engraving, as instanced by the work of Whiting, Myers and others.

11 The portrait head of Queen Victoria on the City of London medal of 1838 by William Wyon RA. *NPM.*

III

The Design and Printing of the One Penny Black

Adhesive postage stamps have been so long a feature of our daily life that it is not easy to take oneself back in time to the month of October 1839 when Rowland Hill, newly appointed to the Treasury, was faced with the task of creating the very first 'adhesive postage label' as part of his scheme for uniform prepaid postage. Later he proudly realised that he had started something of world-wide importance; but at the time Hill was wholly concerned with a specific problem (one of several) which he was determined to resolve to the best of his considerable ability.

Of his many accomplishments and skills, three were particularly relevant to this matter of postage 'labels'. Firstly, as an inventor in his own right he was familiar with the mechanical and legal problems involved in designing and patenting new machines. Secondly, he had, in the early summer of 1839, made a detailed study of printing techniques in connection with his design for a printing press to work on an entirely new, rotary, process. Lastly, he had shown considerable youthful talent as a painter and was firmly convinced that even the most everyday items could be so made that they would be examples of good and artistic design. There could be no more effective vehicle for carrying such a message to the whole population of Britain than the proposed new labels and envelopes. His background and personal beliefs, with the responsibilities of his new office, thus combined to make him the dominant influence in the designing of the new stamps and it is clear that they conformed to his own ideas.

During his first two months in office, Rowland Hill, apart from investigating the working methods of the Post Office from the inside and writing a long memorandum for the Chancellor of the Exchequer on the detailed measures required to introduce Uniform Penny Postage, investigated various technical aspects of what we would now call stamp production. He recorded in his diary seeing the Bank of England's note printing process *('unsuitable for stamps')* on 30th September, consulting Thompson (the craftsman who later engraved the brass plate for the Mulready Envelopes) as to the means of preventing forgery of stamps (on 25th October) and the following day having discussions with nine leading papermakers and stationers. At the end of November he found time to examine the machinery used for embossing revenue 'stamps' at the Stamping Office (of the Inland Revenue).

During this time Rowland Hill had also been examining most of the suggestions sent into the Treasury for the competition because, as he noted, the Junior Lords of the Treasury (who should have done the work) had *'set aside'* a very large number of the entries. Unfortunately, he was unable to enlist in this work the help of his new assistant Henry Cole, because Cole himself had submitted a personal entry for the competition which proved to be one of the prize-winners.

As Rowland Hill himself recorded (in his autobiography) *'Meanwhile, the examination of the multitudinous devices for producing inimitable stamps having at length been completed, I was called upon to prepare a minute* [report] *on the whole subject.'* The *'Report on the proposed Franking System'* which Hill sent to the Chancellor of the Exchequer on 6th December 1839, not only commented on the proposals and ideas submitted by the competitors but set out detailed proposals for the alternative methods of prepayment of postage and the reasons why they had been selected. As he stated in his opening paragraph *'Several of the communications* [competition entries] *display much ingenuity and contain many useful suggestions;*

still I am not aware that any plan has been prepared which, however excellent, is, as a whole, fit for adoption. I hope to be able, however by combining the suggestions of many, to propose a plan......'

In his Report Hill examined methodically (and in some cases at considerable length) the necessary technical requirements for postage labels and prepaid 'stamped' stationery which would be secure against forgery, cheap and quick to produce, wholly functional and yet not without artistic merit.

Almost the most important requirement was speed of production of the labels. For the new Uniform Postage scheme to become fully effective, with the minimum additional work for Postmasters and their Staffs, it was essential that almost all prepayment of letters be made by the use of pre-paid stationery (letter sheets and envelopes) or by adhesive labels rather than by the slow method of paying in cash over the counter, followed by handstamping etc of the letter by the Post Office clerk or postmaster. The introduction of Uniform Penny Postage was being clamoured for by the public and in fact only a few months away. There was thus an urgent need for very large supplies of labels and envelopes to be ready in post offices before the day of issue; thereafter there had to be an assured supply of each kind weekly to meet normal demands.

At the same time the proposed labels and stationery 'covers' had to be cheap to produce so that their cost represented only a very small fraction of the price at which they were sold.

These two requirements in effect ruled out many of the otherwise attractive Treasury Competition proposals, a number of which involved printing in two or more colours or embossing, or even a combination of these. This was unfortunate as multi-colour printing and embossing made forgery more difficult and the British Treasury in 1839 (and for several decades after then) was constantly (and even obsessively) afraid that attempts would be made to forge the new labels to the detriment of Her Majesty's revenues. In fact their fears were groundless.

Two of the existing printing processes, letterpress and lithography, were also ruled out because neither offered the required degree of security against forgery nor were they, as processes, suitable in 1840 for speedy printing of millions of identical postage labels in sheets. Hill's earlier contacts with printers had suggested to him, quite rightly as it proved, that only the recess printing process – derived from the making of etchings and perfected by Perkins Bacon and Co.[1] – was likely to meet all his requirements.

In recess printing the design is engraved, by hand, on a master steel die which is then hardened [see illus. 18 on page 19] from which it is transferred by a powerful press to a steel roller. The roller, once hardened, is in its turn used to transfer as many images as necessary on to the steel or copper plate from which the sheets of stamps are actually printed. Each of the many images printed from the plate is identical with the single image which can be printed from the original hand-engraved die. The process described above not only gave great security against forgery but allowed for the making of any number of printing plates each of which could produce over two hundred identical stamps at each impression; large quantities of stamps could thus be printed quickly at an acceptable cost.

The next problem concerned the physical size and arrangement of the prepaid stationery and postage stamps so as to make them convenient and easy for the public to use while meeting Treasury and Post Office requirements for ease of handling, storage and accounting. Finally, the designs selected had to be suitable

---

[1]In fact, the name of the firm was Perkins Bacon and Petch from 1834 to 1852, after which the (more familiar) designation of Perkins Bacon and Co. was used.

for the purpose (in the case of the postage stamps to show that the stamp itself was a receipt indicating that the postal charge on the letter to which it was affixed had been prepaid) and at the same time be dignified and of artistic merit. The one indication that did not need to be put on these, the first postage stamps, was the name of the country as, basically, they were intended for use only within the United Kingdom.

It will be recalled that three new kinds of 'stamps' had been proposed and agreed for the prepayment of postage: adhesive labels, prepaid envelopes and letter sheets, and stamped-to-order stationery. Work on all three sorts of 'stamps' went forward simultaneously between December 1839 and May 1840, but here we are concerned only with the adhesive postage labels; the story of the other 'stamps' is told in Chapters IV and VII.

Considering that Rowland Hill was embarking on the design and manufacture of something entirely new it is remarkable that he was able to put forward, as early as 6th December 1839, such very detailed and workable proposals for approval by the Treasury Board. So practical indeed that the proposals – as will be seen – were carried out almost without modification to produce the 1840 adhesive stamps which in turn set the pattern to be followed by most of the world's postage stamps.

Briefly, Hill proposed 'appliqués' in the form of *'small stamps,' 'to be attached to the letter......by means of a glutinous wash at the back.'* The printed part of the stamp was to consist of an (engraved) head of the Queen, *'together with the price of the stamp, the weight it is intended to frank and a distinctive mark which will be described hereafter – the whole sheet being printed at once from a steel plate.'* Later in the report Hill specified that there should be 240 stamps to the sheet (making each sheet of 1d stamps worth £1) and that the *'distinctive mark'* should consist of combinations of letters of the alphabet *'which would make each stamp slightly different from every other.'* He also proposed, as a further safeguard against forgery the use on each stamp of *'a small watermark, a crown for instance, and on the sheet a larger one forming the words "Post Office".'*

Although he personally thought the idea unnecessary Hill also proposed the issue of Twopence stamps as well as Penny ones, to give the public a choice and see whether there was indeed a demand for both values. There would, he wrote, *'be little difficulty in printing the Twopenny stamps. Dies and plates similar to those employed for the Penny stamps and copied mechanically from the same originals (the figure marking the* [changed] *value being inserted by hand) would suffice; and as a means of readily distinguishing the 1d and 2d stamps, they should be printed in different colours.'* The Twopenny rate of course covered letters weighing ½oz or over and less than 1oz.

Finally, Hill was able to tell the Lords of the Treasury that there would be no difficulty in obtaining sufficient supplies of the adhesive stamps as required. He had already discussed the question of printing with Messrs. Perkins Bacon and Co. and, he stated, they *'are willing to contract to supply the necessary number at a rate not exceeding 8d per 1000 stamps, including* [the making of] *the plates but not including the paper which would probably cost 2d or 3d per thousand more.'*

Producing the Stamp 'Labels'

When it came to carrying out Rowland Hill's proposals (which had been wholly accepted by the Lords of the Treasury) it was Henry Cole, his assistant, who under Hill's supervision, was in charge of the day-to-day negotiations with artists and printers. Rowland Hill himself was almost fully occupied with the formidable task of implementing the reform of the postal system itself.

Hill's report of 6th December had laid down almost all the necessary specifications for the proposed adhesive labels: they should be of small size, printed by recess (engraved) in sheets of 240, on watermarked paper and incorporating in the design itself the head of the Queen and distinctive combinations of letters (as a deterrent to forgery).

One further, and most important, element in the design was probably proposed by J. B. Bacon, whose firm (the printers Perkins Bacon and Co.) had patented a machine – the rose-lathe – which was an improved version of a geometrical lathe used for engine-turning the back of watches. Similar modern machines produce the intricate patterns which form the backgrounds of banknotes. Bacon's proposal to use such engine turning as the background for the main part of the design (the royal portrait) was taken up by Hill and Cole, and incorporated in an agreed specification for the new labels drawn up by J. B. Bacon on 14th December. *'Perkins Bacon,'* he wrote, *'would engage to prepare a die to be composed of the best engraving of Her Majesty's portrait which we can get executed by the best Artist, to be surrounded by white and black engine-turned work – and the appropriate wording – for the sum of seventy-five guineas.'*

The Main Elements of the Design

Perkins Bacon immediately commissioned a drawing (of suitable size) of a profile portrait of the Queen, to be adapted from the head of William Wyon's 1838 City Medal. The artist engaged for this commission was Henry Corbould, a well-known miniaturist and book illustrator, who had recently completed for Perkins Bacon three delightful pencil drawing[1] of the young Queen Victoria which were used for colonial banknotes and also for 'Heath's Book of Beauty.'

12 William Wyon's hand-drawn postage stamp essay believed to have been submitted for the Treasury Competition.
Collection of H.M. The Queen.

13 Essay of December 1839 with hand-painted inscription 'POST OFFICE HALF OUNCE ONE PENNY' on an engine-turned background.
Cole Bequest, Victoria & Albert Museum.

Corbould's portrait drawing for the Penny Black, does not appear to have survived; it was probably officially destroyed soon after May 1840. We do know, however, that it was shown to Henry Cole on 30th December 1839 by J. B. Bacon who later paid Corbould £12 for his work. While this portrait was being completed, Bacon himself was preparing some preliminary designs (in essay form) for the stamps as a whole, which he submitted to Cole at the end of December 1839. Cole kept three of these which all show the head as a white silhouette against various printed engine-turned backgrounds. The most significant of these bears round the head a circular inscription reading: 'POST OFFICE HALF OUNCE ONE PENNY.' It is likely that this wording was added to the basic essay (probably by Cole himself) to convert it into an essay of William Wyon's competition design. Certainly the resemblance is too marked to be merely a coincidence [illus. 13].

[1]Now in the R. M. Phillips Collection in the National Postal Museum.

All the backgrounds had been engraved, on the Perkins rose-lathe, by a master engraver called George Rushall who began his apprenticeship to the craft in 1810 as attested by his original indenture certificate (now in the National Postal Museum). The general design of Bacon's essays must have been approved by Rowland Hill because on 31st December he instructed Perkins Bacon to put along the bottom of the stamp a horizontal inscription reading *'Half oz One Penny'* and at the top, behind the head, *'certain letters to vary with each stamp.'*

Making the Master Die

The most important step in the production of a recess-printed (engraved) postage stamp (such as the 1840 Penny Black) is the creation of the master steel die which is then used to make the actual printing plates. The quality of the printed stamps is as good (or bad) as the master die.

14 Proof from a plate engraved with five impressions each of the rejected first die and the *accepted* background of the second die. *NPM.*

In the case of the Penny Black the most important part of the die was, of course, the portrait of the Queen. First, Cole and J. B. Bacon between them selected an available and – so they thought – suitable engine-turned background (in fact that used for the third of the preliminary essays) and had this rolled (under some 20 tons pressure) into a square piece of soft steel, a space of approximately the right size and shape being left blank for the engraving of the head. The delicate and highly skilled work of engraving was entrusted to Charles Heath who had a considerable reputation for the artistry with which he engraved reproductions of pictures by well known artists. In his work on the Penny Black die Charles Heath was probably greatly assisted by his son Frederick.

In the extraordinary short space of a fortnight, by 15th January 1840, the Heaths had completed the work of engraving on the die the portrait head of the Queen, using as their model Corbould's drawing. They had also engraved along the base the inscription 'POSTAGE ONE PENNY' (an alternative, and shorter version of the wording originally proposed). Unfortunately the proofs of this die showed that it would be unsatisfactory, for the head was too lightly engraved and the engine-turned background equally lacked strength. Another, stronger, background was immediately selected and rolled into a new piece of die steel (again leaving a blank space for the head).

A special printing plate of five impressions from the rejected die, above five impressions of the 'die' with the new background, was made to compare the two 'dies.' A proof in blue printed from this trial plate shows clearly how much better the new die was likely to be [illus. 14]. Though the Heaths received the new background the very same day, on 16th January, the engraving of this second version of the master die took them over a month. But the result was not just satisfactory; it was a miniature masterpiece which set a standard for subsequent engraved postage stamps throughout the world.

Even before the engraving of this (second) die was started the completion and placing on sale to the public of the new adhesive labels and the postal stationery had become a matter of considerable urgency. Popular demand at the end of 1839 had been so insistent that the Government had had to introduce the promised Uniform Penny Postage on 10th January 1840, before either the adhesive labels or the prepaid covers were available. Postage had therefore to be prepaid in cash at Post Offices, which was slow and often inconvenient to the public and was regarded as unsatisfactory by Hill himself, who was naturally anxious to bring *all* his proposals into effect.

The completion of the Penny Black design

While he waited anxiously to see if the new die turned out satisfactorily, Rowland Hill turned his attention to completing the remaining (and more functional) parts of the design. These were: firstly the inscriptions which would indicate the purpose of the new label and its value for prepayment of postage, then the check letters which were intended to make forgery much more difficult and finally the ornaments and frame lines which would complete and lend unity to the whole design.

This work took almost two months (mid-January to 5th March 1840) and involved the closest co-operation between J. B. Bacon, Henry Cole, Edwin Hill (Rowland's brother, who was in charge of stamp printing at the Treasury) and, of course, Rowland Hill himself, who undoubtedly not only made the final decisions but was also certainly the man who contributed most to the final design.

The original inscription *'Half oz One Penny'* had been changed early in January 1840 to *'Postage One Penny'* in one line (as engraved on Heath's original rejected die). Later, probably early in February, two proofs were made from a duplicate of

15 Essay for the inscription and corner lettering of the Penny Black. *V. & A.*

the 'blank head' die (with the new type background) which was in the process of being engraved by the Heaths. These proofs were used to try alternative positions for the necessary inscriptions. To one was added, along the base, the single line inscription previously used. The other was engraved with 'POSTAGE' occupying part of the top and 'ONE PENNY' most of the bottom label. This still left small blank boxes, formed by the frame lines, in the four corners of the design [illus. 15]. Hill had already decided to use these for his scheme of variable check letters.

On 21st February he sent J. B. Bacon a drawing, showing how the check letters should be arranged on a sheet of 240 stamps (20 horizontal rows of 12 stamps) with the 'stamps' lettered – in the top corners – from AA to AL along the top row and so on down the sheet until the 20th row which was lettered TA to TL. This arrangement of check letters continued in use for nearly 40 years.

At first Hill proposed to put letters (inside stars) in all the four corners: the check letters in the upper and 'VR' (Victoria Regina) in the lower corners. This was on 17th February. Before the end of the month he had a better idea which

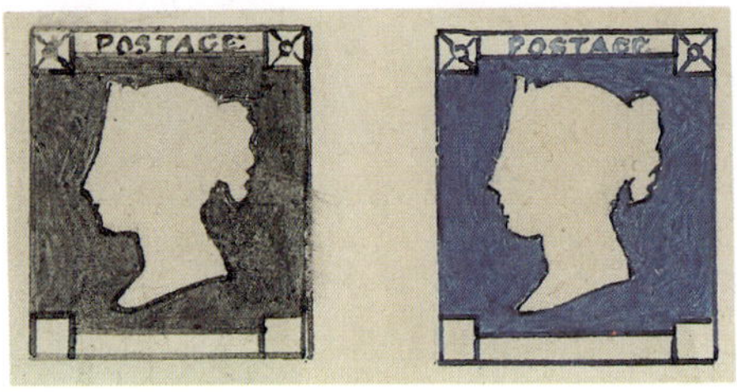

16 Watercolour sketches made to show the effect of putting stars/crosses in the upper corners of the Penny Black design. *NPM.*

was given form in watercolour sketches which he sent to the Chancellor of the Exchequer. These sketches [illus. 16] show a cross in each of the two top corners, the lower corners being left blank for the variable check letters. The design was now complete.

The Heaths finished engraving the head on the second die by 20th February. A proof impression taken at this stage [illus. 17] was shown by the Chancellor of the Exchequer to the Queen, who expressed her *'high appreciation'* of it in a letter. The Heaths then went on to complete the actual Penny die by adding the inscription and the frame lines (4th March) and finally (about 13th March) the crosses in the upper corner. This is the master die [illus. 18] now in the Post Office collection at the National Postal Museum. The inscription 'OLD ORIGINAL' was added some 20 years later.

Making the Printing Plates

On 20th March the Treasury authorised the printers to start making a printing plate for the 1d 'labels' (as well as a die and a printing plate for the 2d value in the same design). Using their special rolling-in process [described on page 13] Perkins Bacon made a plate of 240 impressions and had taken a single proof from it by 1st April [illus. 19 on page 20]. This they sent to Rowland Hill.

This proof was taken from the plate before the check letters were put on and before the marginal inscriptions were engraved on the plate. Rowland Hill sent this first proof sheet to Baring who, having approved it, is believed to have shown it to his Cabinet colleagues. It was then returned to Rowland Hill who kept it with his private papers. When he retired from the Post Office in 1864 Hill took the sheet with him. In 1905 his son Pearson Hill presented it to the Post Office and it is now in the National Postal Museum. The proof of 1st April 1840 is now the only known surviving complete sheet of Penny Blacks.

The final stages of plate making involved the insertion of the check letters in the lower corners and the engraving, along each of the four sides, of the marginal inscriptions – which gave the price of the 'labels' singly as well as per row and per sheet, and also instructions on where the label should be stuck on the folded letter. The engraving of the inscriptions was done by hand but the check letters (480 per sheet) were punched in one by one with a special tool directly onto the metal plate.

17 Proof of the One Penny master die after completion of the Queen's head. *NPM.*

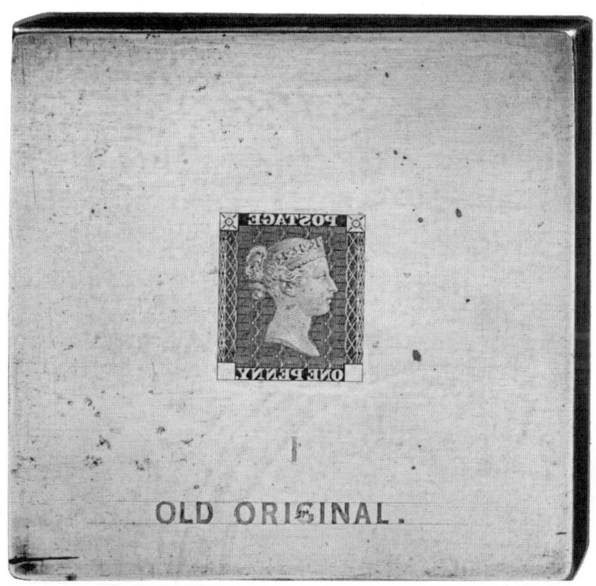

18 The completed original 1840 One Penny master die. *NPM.*

19 The unique 1st April 1840 proof of the first *unfinished* printing plate for the One Penny Black. *NPM.*

Slight differences occurred in the positioning and straightness of the same pair of check letters (say A-A) as between each of the eleven plates from which Penny Blacks were printed. This fact, together with other minute variations, enable philatelists to identify from which plate a stamp with a particular combination of letters was actually printed. This is known as 'plating.' The first Penny Black plate

20 First Day *6th May 1840* cover of the Penny Black used within the City of London. *NPM.*

was completed on 8th April and printing started on 11th April. The One Penny stamps were placed on sale on 1st May and became valid for postage on 6th May 1840 [illus. 20]. Two letters, improperly stamped with Penny Blacks, are known to have been sent through the post as early as 2nd May.

The Twopence Blue

Since it had been decided that Twopenny labels would be required for double weight letters (i.e. over ½oz and under 1oz) and heavy packages such as legal or financial documents, Charles and Frederick Heath started work on a Twopenny master die the very next day following the completion of the Penny die. They were able to use a duplicate impression of their engraved head and background to which they added the inscriptions 'POSTAGE' and 'TWO PENCE' and the frame-lines and crosses as for the one penny die. Though the Heaths finished this die on 8th April plate making was delayed by the priority being given to the One Penny value which it had been announced would be put on sale on 1st May. In fact the Twopence plate was only completed on that date and though actual printing started on 2nd May no copies were put on sale until 8th May, and that in London only [illus. 21].

21 Matched blocks *both from Plate 1* of the 1840 One Penny and Two Pence stamps. *NPM.*

The 'VR' stamp

The issue of the Twopence had also been delayed by the priority given by Rowland Hill to the production of a variant of the One Penny black intended for use by Government Departments on official correspondence; like MPs, the Departments had lost their free franking privileges as part of Hill's reforms. This official stamp was to be distinguished from the ordinary One Penny by having the letters 'VR' in the upper corners (instead of crosses) as well as the normal check letters in the lower corners [illus. 22]. Work on a special 'VR' plate was started late in March 1840 and it was ready for printing by 14th April. Within a month over 3,000 sheets of these 'VR' stamps had been printed but then it was decided not to issue them.

Instead Government Departments, particularly the Tax Offices, were given large surplus stocks of the unpopular Mulready covers [see page 35] to use up.

22 The 'VR' stamp prepared for use by government departments but not issued. These copies bear experimental cancellations. *NPM.*

All the three original postage stamps – the One Penny black, the 'VR' One Penny and the Twopence blue – were printed on special paper watermarked with a small crown. Ever cost-conscious, Rowland Hill and the Excise Office decided that (watermarked) paper made by Stacey Wise of Rush Mills, Northampton, was both cheaper and just as secure as John Dickinson's silk-thread paper (which was in fact used for the Mulready stationery).

The stamps were all gummed at the back ready for use (though the gum was officially described as 'cement'), but the gumming process (brushed onto the sheets by hand) caused much trouble to the printers for several months. The sheets of stamps were not perforated (the first perforated stamps were not to be issued until 1854) and they therefore had to be cut up with scissors. At first care was taken in separating the stamps but after the novelty wore off individual stamps were cut off anyhow and copies with good clear margins became increasingly difficult to find. But with customary Victorian enterprise a private inventor produced in 1840 a mechanical device for cutting up sheets of stamps quickly, which he sold to firms needing large quantities of single stamps.

Finally, the selection of the colours in which the stamps were to be printed. Towards the end of February 1840 the printers, Perkins Bacon, had submitted (probably to Rowland Hill) impressions of the incomplete new die printed in 12 colours including red, blue, brown and black. In an accompanying letter they stated that though they were willing to print the new stamps in any practicable colour, *'we most strongly advise the penny stamp to be printed in black ink, as beyond all comparison superior to any other for steel plate engraving.'* This must have convinced the Treasury because the printing contract awarded to Perkins Bacon on 18th March specified: *'The 1d value to be Black. The 2d to be Blue.'*

The printing of the original 1840 postage stamps, and for that matter their successors in 1841, was carried out by Perkins Bacon & Co. at their works at 69 Fleet Street, London. They were printed on five (later six) flat-bed printing presses [illus. 23 overleaf] specially designed many years earlier by Jacob Perkins (the founder of the firm) for high quality banknote printing. In the hands of skilled printers, each press (which was worked by a large-diameter hand-wheel) was capable of printing some 800 sheets of stamps in 24 hours. In his diary entry for 10th May 1840, Rowland Hill records that *'the demand for labels is such that the contractors (Perkins Bacon), though they now have five presses, are obliged to work night and day; they are now producing 600,000 (stamps) daily.'*

The Penny Black stamps were in production between 11th April 1840 and 3rd February 1841. A total of 11 printing plates were used for the ordinary One Penny Stamps from which Perkins Bacon printed over 68,000,000 stamps in black.

23 The original 1839-40 presses used by Perkins Bacon & Co. to print the 1840 postage stamps.

Printing of the 1840 Twopenny stamps began on 1st May 1840, using the first of two printing plates and continued until 29th August 1840. The total quantity printed from them was less than a tenth of the quantity of the One Penny value: some 6,460,000 stamps in all.

Apart from the preliminary One Penny proof sheet of 1st April, one (or in some cases two) proof sheets were taken from each of the actual printing plates for the 1d and 2d values and formally 'registered' (as suitable and authorised for printing) at the Inland Revenue offices at Somerset House. These are known as 'Imprimatur' or 'Registration' sheets. Unfortunately the Imprimatur sheets of Plates 4, 6, 7, 9, 10 and 11 of the One Penny and both Plates 1 and 2 of the Two Pence disappeared (probably before 1882) while still in the custody of the Inland Revenue. The surviving sheets (less the 20 to 30 stamps which were officially cut off each sheet between 1882 and 1914) are now in the National Postal Museum. Though the two master dies were preserved, the 1840 Plates themselves, in accordance with Treasury policy, were all destroyed by 1843.

As a postscript, it should be recorded that, using the original die and a modern photo-etching process, Messrs. Bradbury Wilkinson & Co. made a replica 1840 One Penny printing plate in December 1978, with the authority of the Post Office. This replica plate was used in February 1979 to print four sheets in black and red on an original 1840 press as part of a BBC Television series 'In the Post.' Two of the sheets were officially destroyed: the plate and the two other facsimile sheets are now part of the Post Office collection in the National Postal Museum.

IV

The Mulready Envelopes and Letter sheets

The method of prepayment most favoured by Rowland Hill, and proposed in his 1837 pamphlet, was the sale to the public of 'stamped covers' to be produced by the Stamp Office (a department of the Inland Revenue). The price of each cover would include the cost of postage so that it could be posted without any further payment.

This form of prepayment had been favoured also by most of the entrants in the Treasury Competition of August 1839. When Rowland Hill reported to the Chancellor of the Exchequer on that competition he made his own very definite recommendations for stamped (prepaid) stationery. He proposed that his 'covers' (or letter sheets) should *'be of the size of half a sheet of quarto letter-paper, namely 9" x 7½". The paper to be of rather inferior quality for the sake of cheapness, with a watermark ("Post Office") across the middle. To have the most beautiful design that can be obtained engraved in relief, with the addition of certain engine etc work and printed in such a manner that when the cover is folded the design shall form a border round its face, with the Queen's head at the back just below the seal.'*
The rough pencil sketch of such a cover which he attached to the report may have been drawn by Hill himself. More probably it was the work of Henry Cole (both men were artists) who recorded in his diary entry for 5th December *'very busy at the Treasury making a design for an envelope'* [illus. 24 overleaf]. This design introduces the allegorical spirit in which Hill no doubt hoped the designs would be executed. While accepting that such a design *('which is intended to serve the purpose of a stamp')* could not be made very difficult of imitation, Hill considered that the watermark and the low cost (1/5th of a penny each to print) of the cover, compared to the cost of production to the forger, would afford ample security.

Hill also showed his far-sightedness by recommending the printing of 'stamped' pieces of paper of a lozenge form for making up into envelopes. These would need only half as much paper as a letter sheet and therefore should be no more expensive when made up by hand as complete envelopes (by the stationers) than the letter sheets. Until this time envelopes had been a luxury used mainly for social purposes by the aristocracy and the rich. Their lack of popular usage was due to the fact that the Post Office letter charges were partly based on the number of 'sheets' and that an envelope counted as a 'sheet'. Envelopes were more convenient to use than folded letters and since, as a result of Hill's postal reforms, their use no longer automatically increased the postage charge, they became extremely popular almost overnight. The dramatic leap in popular demand for envelopes is evidenced by a letter written by the stationers and printers Thomas De La Rue (probably to Henry Cole) on 11th March 1841: *'In reply to your enquiries we beg to say that previously to the Reduction of Postage very few envelopes were in use - since then our consumption goes on increasing - latterly we sell about 40,000 per day - we can hardly however supply regularly our demand or we should be selling more.'* At the Great Exhibition of 1851 De La Rue showed a machine (of which Edwin Hill was part inventor) on which one workman could make 2,500 envelopes an hour, and the envelope had taken over. For convenience the term 'cover' is used hereafter to include both envelopes and letter sheets.

Rowland Hill's proposal to introduce a 'stamped' prepaid envelope was first given practical form on 16th January 1840. This was six days after the introduction of Uniform Penny Postage and the loss (under the Postage Act of 1839) by all Members of Parliament, of their privilege of franking letters. After discussions

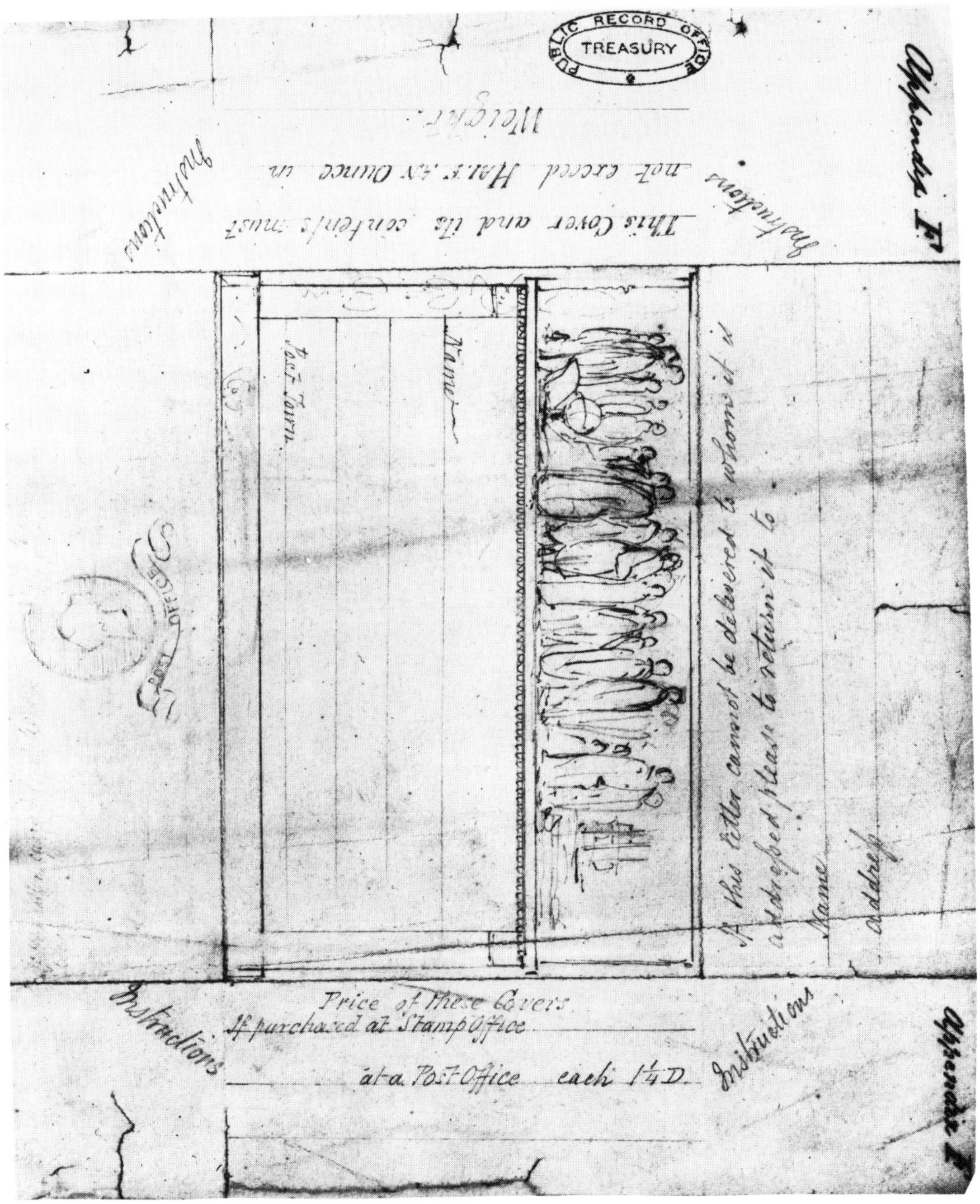

24 The design for a pre-paid letter sheet *probably by Henry Cole* attached to Rowland Hill's Report of 6th December 1839. *Public Record Office.*

with Parliamentary officials, Hill arranged to provide rather plain prepaid envelopes, free of charge, to Members of both Houses, which would go postage free provided they were posted in the respective Houses of Parliament [illus. 25]. The supply of these envelopes ceased with the putting on sale of the Post Office prepaid covers on 1st May 1840.

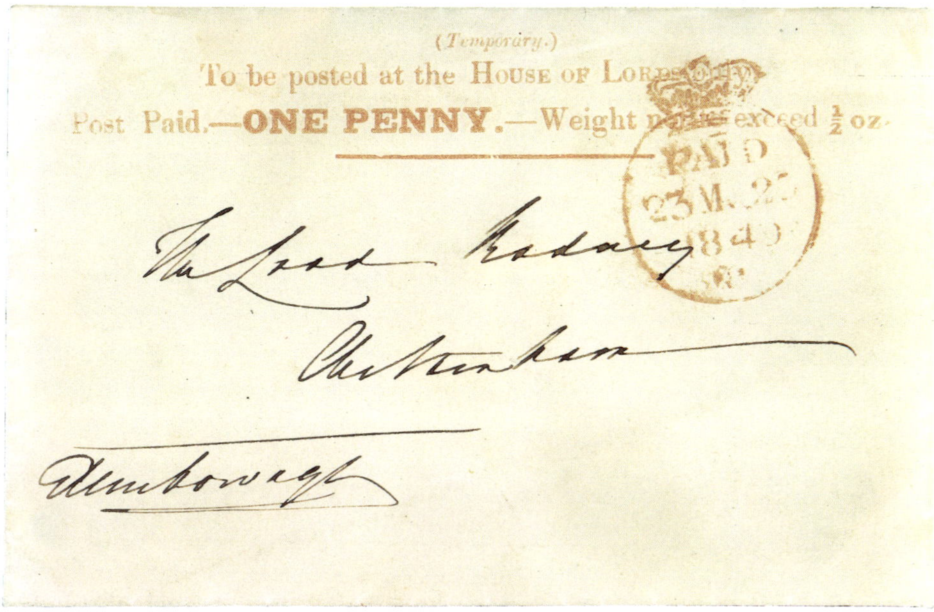

25 Prepaid 'House of Lords' envelope used on 23rd March 1840. *NPM.*

Rowland Hill charged his assistant Henry Cole with the task of obtaining a design for the 'Post Office' covers. Hill himself, at the end of 1839, was very fully occupied in working out the details of how Uniform Penny Postage was to be introduced – the more so as he was not receiving much co-operation from the officials of the Post Office. Thanks to the diaries kept by both Cole and Hill one can trace the sequence of events in some detail. On 29th November we find Cole noting that John Thompson, the engraver, had come to him to *'discuss envelope design and brought some hints for subjects.'* On 7th December, Cole received a visit from the well-known artist, Henry Corbould, who was also interested in designing the projected covers. Corbould worked quickly and four days later produced his envelope design [illus. 26 overleaf].

This design cannot have been what Rowland Hill was looking for because on 12th December Cole went to see Sir William Mulready RA whose name had been suggested to Hill by Mr. Francis Baring, the Chancellor of the Exchequer. Four days later Cole wrote that he had again called on Mulready *'who had made a highly poetic design for the envelope. Took it to Rowland Hill who seemed to like it,'* [see illus. 27 on page 29]. If, as has been suggested, Hill had prepared a note outlining his own ideas for Cole to give Sir William, then it is not surprising that

26 Sketch by Henry Corbould for a pre-paid letter sheet, rejected in favour of the Mulready design. *V. & A.*

Mulready's design pictures the benefits soon to be brought by Uniform Penny Postage. This design was approved by Baring on 4th January 1840.

Since Mulready's 'poetic' design had to be printed cheaply and (it was expected) in very large quantities it was decided to use a printing process known as polytyping, the design etc being printed from metal blocks made from a hand-engraved original die. The paper selected for the Mulready covers was one made by John Dickinson which incorporated, as an anti-forgery measure, coloured silk threads embedded in the texture of the paper. In spite of Cole's industry and energy, the pace of the operation depended on John Thompson, the engraver. Thompson had made his reputation as an engraver on wood and one must surmise that he found working on the brass die of the Mulready design much more difficult. Whatever the reason it took almost exactly three months for Thompson to send the first proofs to Rowland Hill and Baring, on 1st April 1840, which in the event, proved to be a singularly appropriate date. In his diary (2nd April), Rowland Hill noted that *'Mr. Baring is much pleased with the stamp for the covers.'* So much so that the very next day the Chancellor of the Exchequer wrote to Queen Victoria to lay before her *'a proof of the new Post Office envelope'*; he also enclosed a memorandum in which each artist explained his work. The design was, in Mulready's own words, *'intended to convey the idea that the measure it assists in carrying out emanates from Great Britain, and that it is a very widespreading benefit, facilitating our friendly and commercial intercourse with remote lands, and bringing, in a manner, our separated brethren closer to the sick beds and cheerful firesides of home.*'[1] Ten days later proofs of the covers were *'much approved'* by the full Council of the Royal Academy.

In spite of such eminent scrutiny of the design and the close watch which Mulready and Thompson himself had given the brass die during the long process of engraving, everyone missed the fact that one of the angels (at the top right of the design) only had one foot; and the design was printed and issued in that form.

With less than a month to go before the covers and the adhesive stamps were due to be put on sale speed of production was all important. All the more so as it had been decided to print the letter sheets and envelopes in both 1d and 2d values. Printing started on 14th April, under the close supervision of Edwin Hill, who was a gifted engineer and had been appointed Inspector of Stamping at Somerset House on 31st January 1840. On 15th April Henry Cole was able to write to Mulready *'My dear Sir, these are specimens of the real thing now printing at the rate of seventy thousand per hour.'* The enclosure was a Two Pence letter sheet.

The Mulready covers raised a cancellation problem – how to prevent fraudulent re-use. The use of existing postal markings, struck anywhere, would be insufficient once the adhesive stamps became available. Rowland Hill's solution was quite simple and effective. He suggested to the Secretary of the Post Office that the appropriate postal officials be instructed to use the new cancelling handstamps to strike a 'Maltese Cross' cancel on the figure of Britannia in the centre of the design. *'If the Britannia,'* he wrote, *'were always struck it would be fair to assume that a label (stamp) placed over the Britannia was put there to cover the obliterative stamp and to charge (postage due) accordingly.'*

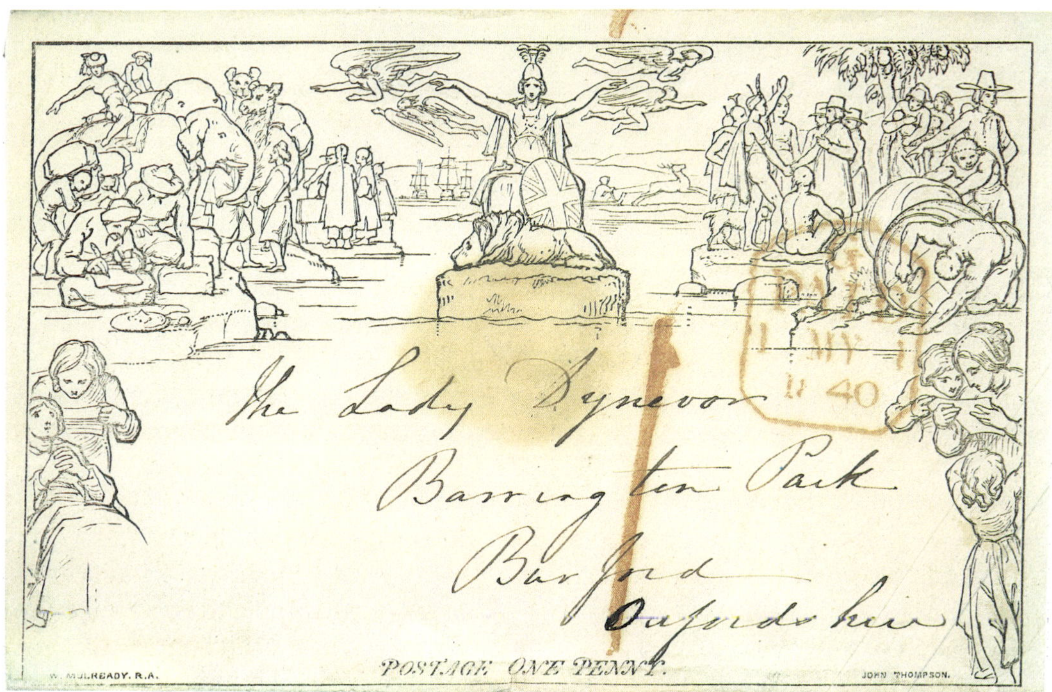

27 A Mulready cover used on 1st May 1840 from London. *NPM.*

The Mulready covers, which were placed on sale on 1st May 1840 were valid for use and pre-payment of postage as from 6th May (the same dates as the Penny Black). The earliest day of use recorded for any Mulready stationery is 1st May for a One Penny envelope, but on this example [illus. 27] pre-payment has had to be made in cash.

---

[1] Quoted by gracious permission, from the original letter and memorandum of 3rd April 1840 in the Royal Library, Windsor Castle.

Although, as will be seen, the new stationery with its artistic and educative design was severly criticised, some users must have appreciated Rowland Hill's good intentions and went to the trouble of hand-colouring the printed design – the result being usually most attractive [illus. 28]. A Two Pence envelope bearing a strip of five of the adhesive Two Pence blue stamps to prepay the one shilling rate from Bristol to Malta in November 1840 is probably one of the most spectacular Mulready items known [illus. 29]. It does however show clearly the limitations of One Penny or even Two Pence stamps and stationery for the prepayment of letters going overseas and therefore liable to larger rates of postage.

28 Hand-coloured Mulready envelope posted from London in June 1840. *NPM.*

29 Two Pence Mulready envelope to Malta, with a strip of five Twopence blue adhesive stamps to make up the One Shilling postage rate. *NPM.*

V

The First Cancellations

The creation and imminent introduction of adhesive postage stamps raised the important question of how these adhesives should be cancelled or (to use the term then current) 'destroyed.' Such cancellation would be necessary when a letter, with a stamp (or stamps) affixed to indicate prepayment of postage, passed through the Post Office, in order to show that the stamp had served its purpose and to prevent it being re-used.

The need to cancel adhesive postage labels had been foreseen by James Chalmers as early as February 1838, while in 1839 Chalmers and several other entrants showed cancellations as part of their submissions to the Treasury Competition.

However, none of these suggestions were taken up. When the method of cancellation was considered officially – both at the Treasury and in the Post Office – in February 1840 there proved to be several schools of thought. The first, represented by Rowland Hill himself, favoured the use of Post Office datestamps. This eminently sensible proposal was turned down, possibly for the petty reason that Colonel Maberley, the Secretary of the Post Office, opposed almost every suggestion which came from Hill at the Treasury.

Hill tried again, in September 1840 when, after pointing out some of the defects of the existing (Maltese Cross) cancellor – and the waste of man-hours used in the double operation of applying both a cancellation *and* a datestamp to each letter – he proposed the use of an extra large double datestamp. This proposal, too. was ignored by the Post Office until the mid-1850s.

The second alternative to be considered was the use of one or other of the various implements suggested by members of the public, which damaged the actual surface of the stamps. None proved suitable. Some did not obliterate sufficiently strongly; some were mechanically faulty or too slow or expensive for general use. Others (such as a leather punch) inevitably damaged the letter underneath the stamp. Another, somewhat similar, proposal was to have the adhesive label placed across the flap or closure of the envelope like a seal so that it had to be destroyed by the act of opening the letter. But this method was not proof against dishonesty.

The Maltese Cross

The practical (but time-wasting) method of obliteration actually adopted was the use of a 'dumb' cancellor (the 'Maltese Cross') on the adhesive stamps (which should have prevented any fraudulent second usage), together with a Post Office named date-stamp struck on the cover itself.

The Maltese Cross design of May 1840 must be the best known cancellation in the world; partly, no doubt, because it was the very first one of all, but partly also because it is so distinctive and attractive. Some doubts have been expressed as to whether this standard-type cancellor issued to most Postmasters about 20th April 1840 has been correctly named by philatelists (the Post Office used no descriptive name). English heraldic usage is to call any cross in which the arms of the cross become broader as they leave the centre a 'cross patée.' The French, on the other hand, call a cross of this type with squared ends to the arms a 'croix de Malte.'
It has been suggested that the 1840 cancellation was a combination of the cross patée and a four-petalled Tudor rose.

A real mystery nevertheless, surrounds the origin of the design. Neither Hill nor Cole mention cancellations in their diaries before the end of April 1840. It is almost certain that the 'Maltese Cross' cancelling handstamp was conceived and designed in the Post Office itself. The actual design proposed is shown by three impressions

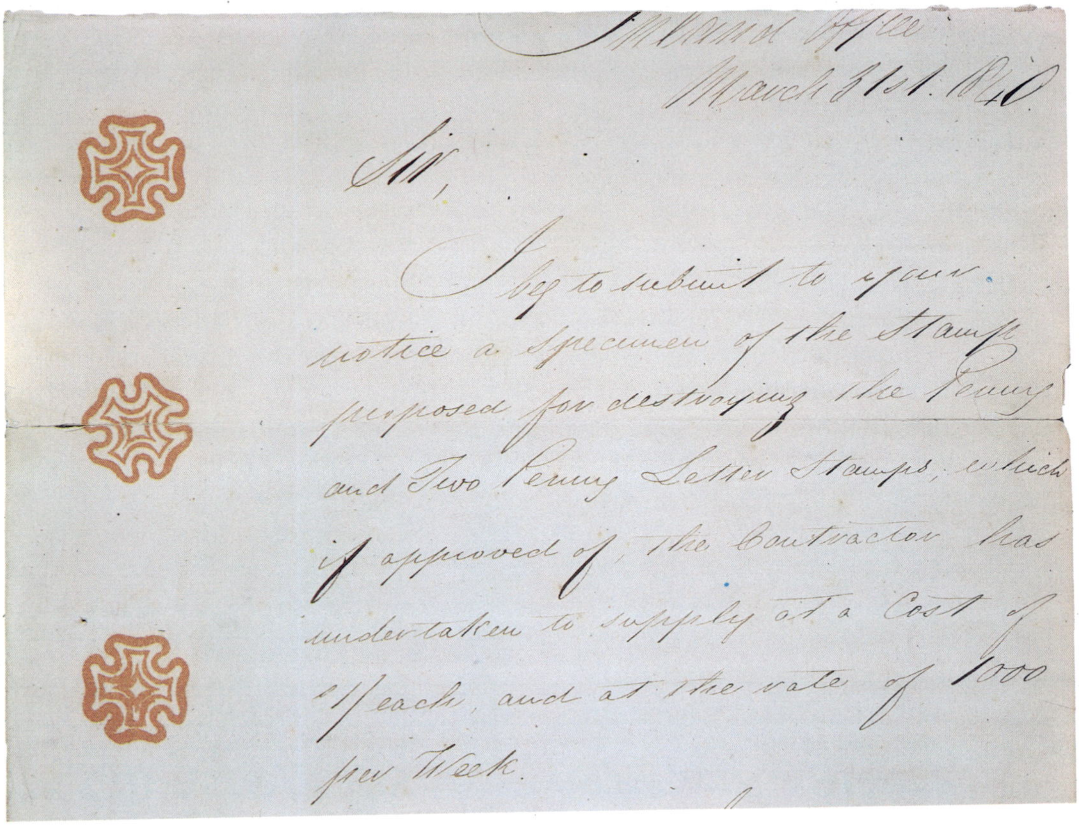
Inland Office
March 31st. 1840

Sir,

I beg to submit to your notice a Specimen of the Stamp proposed for destroying the Penny and Two Penny Letter Stamps, which if approved of, the Contractor has undertaken to supply at a Cost of 1/ each, and at the rate of 1000 per Week.

30 Three proof impressions of the Maltese Cross 'obliterator' on a Post Office minute of 31st March 1840. *NPM.*

in bright red ink of the Maltese Cross in the margin of a minute written by William Bokenham (Superintending President) of the Inland Office of the GPO to the Secretary of the Post Office, on 31st March [illus. 30]. Bokenham wrote: *'I beg to submit to your notice specimens of the stamps proposed for destroying the One Penny and Two Penny Letter Stamps which, if approved of, the Contractors have undertaken to supply at a cost of 1/- each and at the rate of 1,000 per week.'* But not a hint of why this design was selected or by whom. I suggest, however, that since this is an internal Post Office minute and the 'obliteration' (cancellation) of the stamps would have to be undertaken by Postmasters and their clerks, that the design was the work of someone in the Inland Office – possibly Bokenham himself. Two thousand handstamps were ordered and issued in April 1840 but only one example (from a small Post Office in Suffolk) appears to have survived to the present day.

It was a matter of great concern to Rowland Hill and the Treasury that the colour (and composition) of the ink to be used with the handstamps should be selected mainly to ensure that it could not be fraudulently removed from used stamps. The printers, Perkins Bacon, because of their special knowledge of printing inks, were obviously involved in experiments to find the most suitable ink. On 19th March 1840 they sent 12 impressions of a handstamp to Professor Richard Phillips (a Chemist and a Fellow of the Royal Society) for which they had used a red ink *'which we think he cannot extract without taking away paper also.'* Their letter also noted that they had found it possible to remove all kinds of black ink which they had tried. Of course black ink was in any case unsuitable for use on a black stamp – the colour already agreed for the One Penny value.

Rowland Hill recommended the use of this special red ink to Colonel Maberley and called his attention (on 24th April) to the power of creosote to wash out another red ink which the Post Office proposed to use for its Maltese Cross 'obliterator'. Nevertheless, on the following day a Post Office circular was sent to all postmasters bearing a specimen impression of the cancellation and instructing them to make the 'Red Stamping Composition' as follows:

> '1lb Printers red ink
> 1 pint linseed oil
> Half-pint of the droppings of Sweet Oil,
> to be well mixed'

Inevitably, in practice this mixture varied considerably and some country Post Offices used colours other than red for the ink [illus. 31]. So the cancellation can be found in many shades of red and even in colours such as brown (Kensington), bright violet (Market Street), bright blue (Truro), and orange (Liverpool).

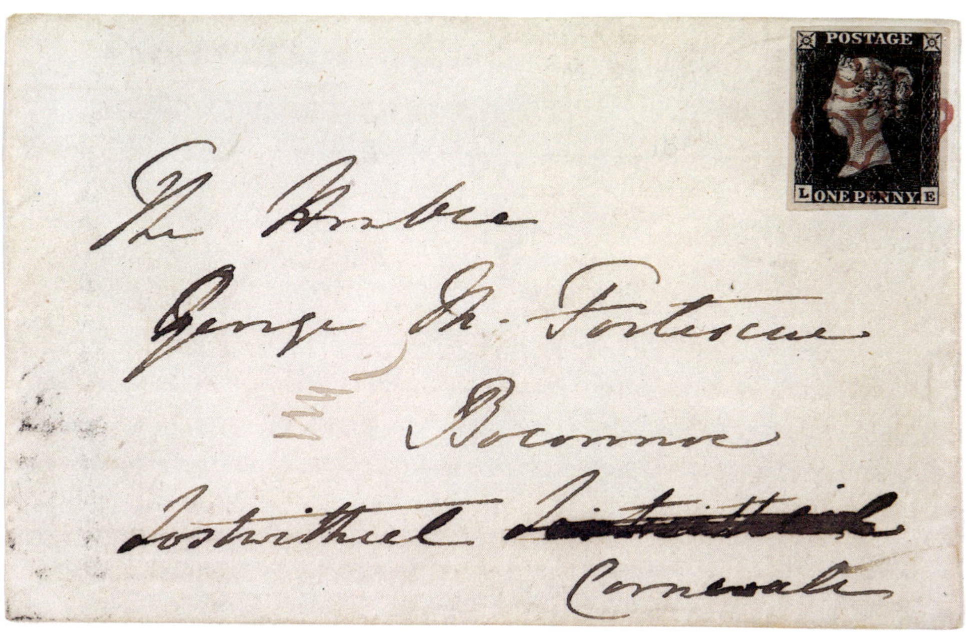

Bright violet *Market Street, Herts.*

Brown *Kensington.*

Orange *Liverpool.*

Blue *Truro.*

31 The Maltese Cross cancellation struck in abnormal colours. *NPM.*

Similarly, since accidental loss or damage or wear made replacements necessary, the actual patterns of some Maltese Cross cancellors are noticeably different from the normal, which suggests that the replacements were locally made.

Illustrated [32] are some of the most distinctive of these local variants: Wotton-under-Edge (Gloucester) which has seven file cuts across the face of the cross, Alderney, Hollymount and Mullingar (Ireland).

Wotton-under-Edge *Gloucester.*

Hollymount.

Alderney.

Mullingar *Ireland.*

32 Local variants of the Maltese Cross cancellation. *NPM.*

Official Post Office instructions laid down that the adhesive stamp(s) should be stuck on the top right hand corner of the letter (this is also stated in the marginal inscriptions of the sheets of stamps) and each stamp cancelled with a single impression of the handstamp. So most Penny and Twopenny stamps used in 1840 were cancelled in such a way that the impression of the cross fell across the Queen's face. But some Post Offices (particularly in the West Country) consistently used their town name and date stamps instead of the Maltese Cross [illus. 32] and other Post Offices occasionally used other available handstamps. The Maltese Cross handstamps were replaced by a new pattern containing numerals in 1844.

VI

Tribulations and Trials

Part 1 Political Attacks and Lampoons

When the One Penny adhesive label (stamp) and the Mulready covers were put on sale in London on 1st May 1840, the adhesive stamps were eagerly welcomed by the public which bought 600,000 One Penny stamps in London on the first day.

The reception given to the Mulready covers was, however, most discouraging. Like the stamps, the covers were the bye-products of a postal reform brought in by a Liberal (Whig) government. Mulready's 'artistic' but somewhat fanciful design was therefore a natural target for Tory criticism and lampoons. The attack started in *The Times* on 2nd May. The editor of that mouthpiece of the Tory party was quick to print a letter from a reader (who enclosed one of the new envelopes) and asked *'Sir. Is it possible that the enclosed is not a fake? After the public have been waiting six months in order that the great "artists" might produce something "worthy of the country" can this be the result? Pray be kind enough, Sir, to inform us whether this piece of nonsensical buffoonery is really genuine?*

Yours etc. A LOVER OF THE FINE ARTS.'

The same newspaper gleefully took the opportunity (also on 2nd May) to embarrass the Liberal government further with a savage editorial attack on Mulready's design. *'We have been favoured'* *The Times* proclaimed *'with a sight of one of the new stamp covers, and we must say that we never beheld anything more ludicrous than the figure or allegorical device by which it is marked with its official character – why not add embellished......It is apparently a spirited attempt to imitate the hieroglyphic which formed one of the ornaments to Moore's Almanac: Britannia is seated in the centre with the lion couchant (Whigish) at her feet, her arms are distended scattering little flying children to some elephants on the left, and on the right to a group of gentlemen......writing on their knees, evidently on account of a paucity of tables.'*

There was much more in the same vein and again on 4th May when a further *Times* editorial apologised for having omitted in its previous remarks on the new postage envelope, *'all mention of one group of figures, which, on close examination, we are convinced the artist must have intended should represent one of the distinguishing characteristics of the Ministry by which this great boon (not the envelopes) has been conferred upon the educated part of the community. We allude to four knowing-looking personages who are standing on the left-hand side of this truly graphic picture......an admirable sketch of three members of the "thimble rig" fraternity......'*

Mulready's Britannia and her attendant lion couchant were also natural targets for *The Times* (and others). *'In conclusion, we must say that the lion is most unlike our all English lions. He appears as sulky, as hungry, and as discontented as a Whig out of place......As to Britannia, she looks as melancholy as if the loss sustained in the Post Office revenue was to be deducted from her pin-money......'*

Which was not entirely unfair as, in fact, the change to Uniform Penny Postage *did* put the Post Office accounts into the red for several years.

It is, of course, possible that had a Tory government happened to have sponsored the new covers, the verdict of *The Times*, and its Tory correspondents might have been less unfavourable!

Even the poets and the versifiers could not resist poking fun at Mulready's design. Thomas Hood, in his long and rambling ditty 'Miss Kilmansegg and her Precious Leg', wrote:

'So the cards were sent for that sort of mob
Where Tarters and Africans hob-and-nob
And the Cherokee talks of his cab and cob
To Polish and Lapland lovers –
Cards, like that hieroglyphical call
To a geographical Fancy Ball
On the present Post Office covers.'

And in one of 'The Ingoldsby Legends' by Richard Barham may be found the following lines:

'The Manager rings, and the Prompter springs
To his side in a jiffy, and with him he brings
A set of those odd-looking envelope things
Where Britannia (who seems to be crucified) flings
To her right and her left funny people with wings
Amongst Elephants, Quakers and Catabaw Kings......'

Mulready was also fair game for the anonymous ballad-writers. One such ballad, published in a newspaper, started off as follows:

'Britannia is sending her messengers forth
To the east, to the west, to the south, to the north,
At her feet is a lion wot's taking a nap
And a dish-cover rests on her legs and her lap.'

But what really killed Mulready's stamped covers were the caricatures. The first and most famous of these was drawn and engraved by John Leech and published (as an envelope) by Fores of Piccadilly, well before the end of May 1840.
The illustration [33] speaks for itself; every feature of the original drawing has been ridiculed, with many anti-Whig overtones such as the allusion to the unpopular Opium War with China. Leech and John Doyle were but the most famous of many artists whose caricatures [illus. 34] so quickly lowered the previously undoubted reputation of William Mulready RA.

Regretfully, Rowland Hill noted on 12th May (in his diary): *'I fear we shall be obliged to substitute some other stamp for that designed by Mulready, which is abused and ridiculed on all sides...... The conduct of the public shows that although our attempts to diffuse a taste for fine art may have been imprudent, such diffusion is very much wanted. I am already turning my attention to the substitution of another stamp, combining with it, as the public have shown their disregard and even distaste for beauty, some further economy in the production.'*

Henry Cole, writing many years later, had to admit that *'After forty years' additional experience, I agree in the soundness of the public opinion expressed, that this fine design was quite unsuitable for its purpose...... The postage cover was for a dry commercial use, in which sentiment has no part.'*

But Rowland Hill's attempts to introduce art into correspondence were not entirely in vain. The Mulready caricatures were swiftly followed by a host of attractive pictorial envelopes for use on special occasions or when writing to special persons [illus. 35 to 37 overleaf].

33 John Leech's May 1840 caricature of the Mulready cover. *NPM.*

34 Mulready caricature number 3 *artist unknown* published by William Spooner. *NPM.*

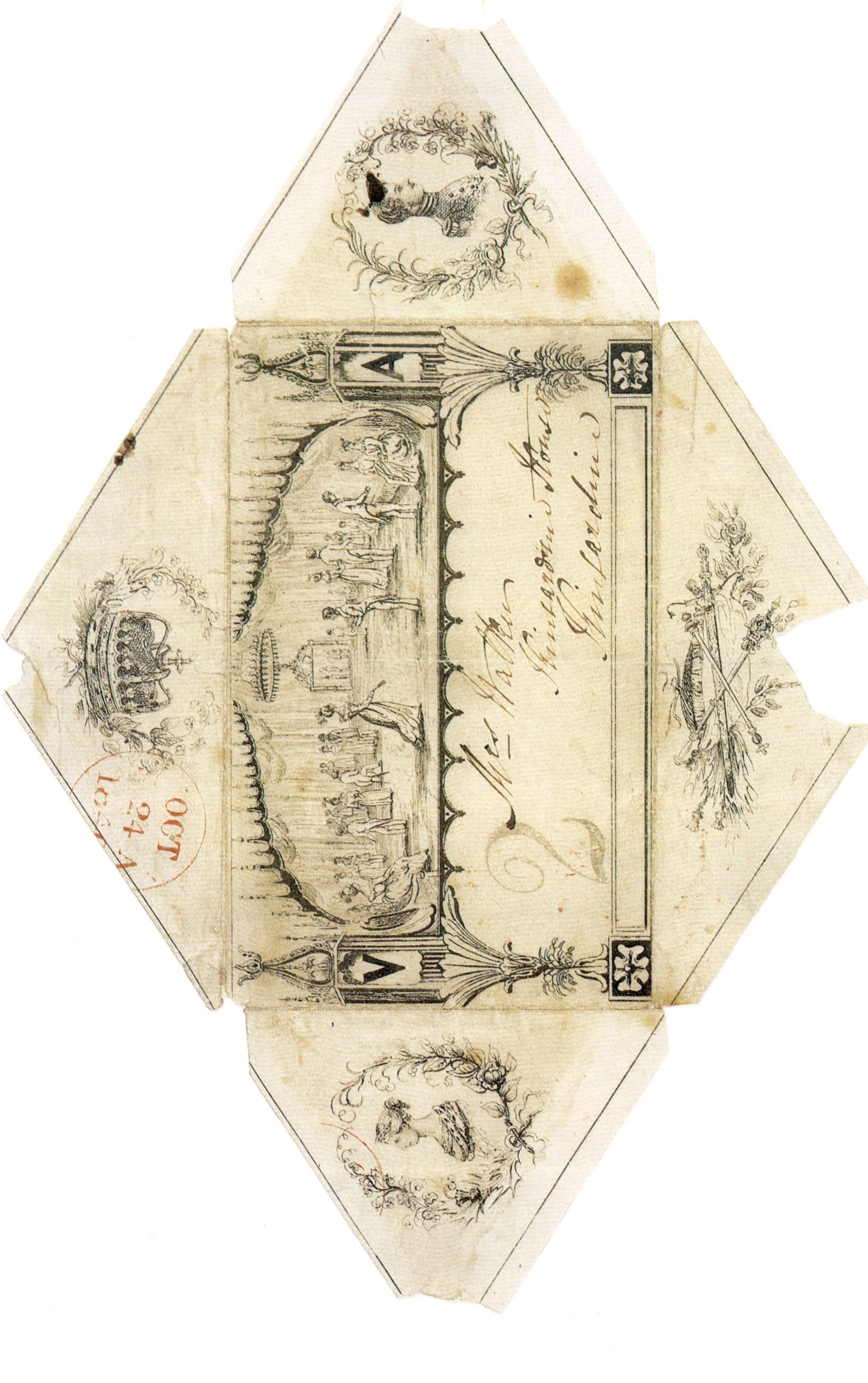

35 The 'Victoria and Albert' pictorial envelope, reputed to have been used to send out invitations to a ball at Holyrood House, Edinburgh, in October 1840. *NPM.*

36 Fore's Coaching Envelope used in October 1840. *NPM.*

37 Fore's Civic Envelope with the statues of Gog and Magog, and the Lord Mayor of London riding on a turtle. *NPM.*

The unsuitable nature of the design and the poor quality of printing, however, were probably not the principal reasons for the public's undoubted preference for the adhesive stamps instead. Hill was mistaken in thinking that the 'stamped' envelopes would be used in the majority of cases. It soon became obvious that far fewer covers were likely to be used than adhesive stamps (or prepayment in cash) because the covers were sold by town booksellers at a profit (it being difficult to procure them in villages and small towns), because they were more trouble than the stamps and because the weight of the covers or envelopes could, not infrequently, increase the cost of postage on a long letter.

The adhesive Penny Black stamp did not escape its share of criticism but, since most of it was politically motivated and artistically unwarranted, it soon died out. *The Times,* as might be expected, led the attack. An 'Engraver and Printer,' in a letter dated 2nd May declared: *'Look, Sir, at the adhesive stamp; it is a libel upon the fair countenance of our Queen – a libel prima facie; and who would be surprised were Prince Albert to indict the perpetrators of so vile an offence to his royal consort? To compare this production, in point of execution, with the fair sultanas that grace the Macassar-oil bottles of Mr. Rowland* [a punning reference to the then popular dressing for men's hair] *would be invidious, for it is inferior......to the heads of Hippocrates and Galen that decorate the quack nostrums......of the licensed poisoners* [the patent medicine makers]......'

A scandal weekly *The Town,* edited (often from prison) by one Nickolson, carried on 6th June the following *'Lines on the Post Office Medallion':*

> *'You must kiss our fair Queen, or her pictures, that's clear*
> *Or the gummy medallion will never adhere;*
> *You will not kiss her hand, you will readily find*
> *But actually kiss little Vickey's behind.'*

There were numerous other attacks on the Penny Black: rival printers claimed that both stamps and envelopes could be easily imitated, a Cheltenham doctor declared that a clerk who was a patient of his had become ill from licking the gum on the stamps, and the *Manchester News* disapproved strongly of the defacement, by the cancellation, of the Queen's portrait.[1] Perhaps the most pardonable criticism of the adhesive stamp came in a letter sent to a lady in Camberwell on 5th May 1840 by an old man of 91 years. Enclosing a Penny Black, he wrote: *'My dear Floral Friend. To make you stare I send you a Queen's head, the day before it is in Penny circulation......what a pity they should make Victoria "gummy" like an old woman without teeth – as I am!'.*

Part 2 Preventing Fraud: The 'Rainbow' Trials

Despite these criticisms there was no doubting the popularity of the adhesive stamps for practical use. Hill wrote in his diary on 1st May *'Stamps issued to the public today (in London) for the first time. Great bustle at the Stamp Office';* on 6th May *'Stamps came into use today. Cole went to the Post Office, reports that about half the letters were stamped.'*

Popular indeed but not, unfortunately, proof against dishonesty. The danger to the revenue was not that of forgery, though Hill later admitted that he had begun to fear imitations because the hasty printing led to some inaccurate and poorly

---

[1] For the early stamps of Sicily and Spain special frame-like cancellations were devised which, carefully applied, did not insult the respective monarch by defacing the royal portraits.

finished stamps. In fact, as he recorded in his autobiography, only two (rather bungling) attempts at forgery were made during the life of the stamps. The author of one was detected because he was a young Irishman who, writing to his sweetheart, used one forged stamp on his letter and enclosed a second for her reply.

The main anxiety came from the difficulty of making the obliteration of the stamps complete and permanent. Only eight days after the stamps started being used Hill recorded that *'the obliteration of the stamps as they pass through the PO appears to be done very carelessly.'* However, before very long the postal clerks. and sorters had become much more practiced and only negligible numbers of stamps escaped obliteration in passing through the Post Office.

The real danger, as Hill saw it, lay in deliberate attempts by dishonest persons to re-use cancelled postage stamps. He wrote in his diary on 21st May 1840 that *'all sorts of tricks are being played by the public who are exercising their ingenuity in devising contrivances for removing the obliterating stamps by chemical agents and other means.'* One ingenious but rarely practised fraud was to take the (complementary) uncancelled halves of two used stamps and join them on a letter to make one apparently unused stamp. Another mentioned by Hill was to wash over the (unused) stamp on the letter, before it was posted, with a varnish such as isinglass which, together with the cancellation, could later be removed with soap and water by the recipient. As for the 'chemical agents' mentioned by Hill, they ranged from water, soap, bread and other materials found in every household, to other substances easily obtainable at the local apothecary's or local printers. These included creosote, turpentine, eucalyptus, linseed and castor oils, as well as chloride of lime, potash, and prussic and tartaric acids. Between them these substances softened, disrupted, or dissolved nearly all types of ink then in use. Some, unfortunately, removed only the red cancelling ink.

On 21st May Hill wrote in his diary: *'I am making every effort......with the aid of Phillips the chemist and others to prevent these frauds and I trust I shall succeed.'* Finding the solution was no easy matter, it occupied much of Hill's time over the next six months and required the co-operation of all the most eminent chemists in England and Ireland including even the redoubtable Michael Faraday.

The trials were conducted on 'stamps' printed from a printing plate of only twelve impressions specially made from the One Penny die; the printed impression of the upper right corner of each stamp being made void either by filling those parts of the plate with wax or by actually defacing it. This was to prevent any examples being used on letters. Because of the wide variety of colours (black, blue, lilac-rose and various shades of green and red) in which these 'stamps' were printed they have been known since 1863 as 'Rainbow' Trials [illus. 38 overleaf].

Reporting to the Chancellor of The Exchequer on the experiments (on 17th September) Hill stated that he had *'assumed that the only practical deviation from the present plan was to alter the colour and composition of the inks now employed in printing the Postage Labels and in obliterating them in transit through the Post Office. The desirability of an immediate solution manifestly precluded all plans which involved any changes in either the plates or the paper now in use.'*

The May – December 'Rainbow' Trials experiments follow – as might be expected of Hill – a logical pattern. The first problem was to find a secure obliterating (cancelling) ink. This proved to be BLACK printer's letterpress ink (although even this required some modification). The use of a black cancelling ink, while reasonable for the blue Twopence stamp, would not be really suitable if the black colour was retained for printing the One Penny stamp: a new colour (or colours) had therefore to be selected. Having selected red for the 1d value (it was decided to keep blue for the 2d), suitable new printing inks for both values had to be devised.

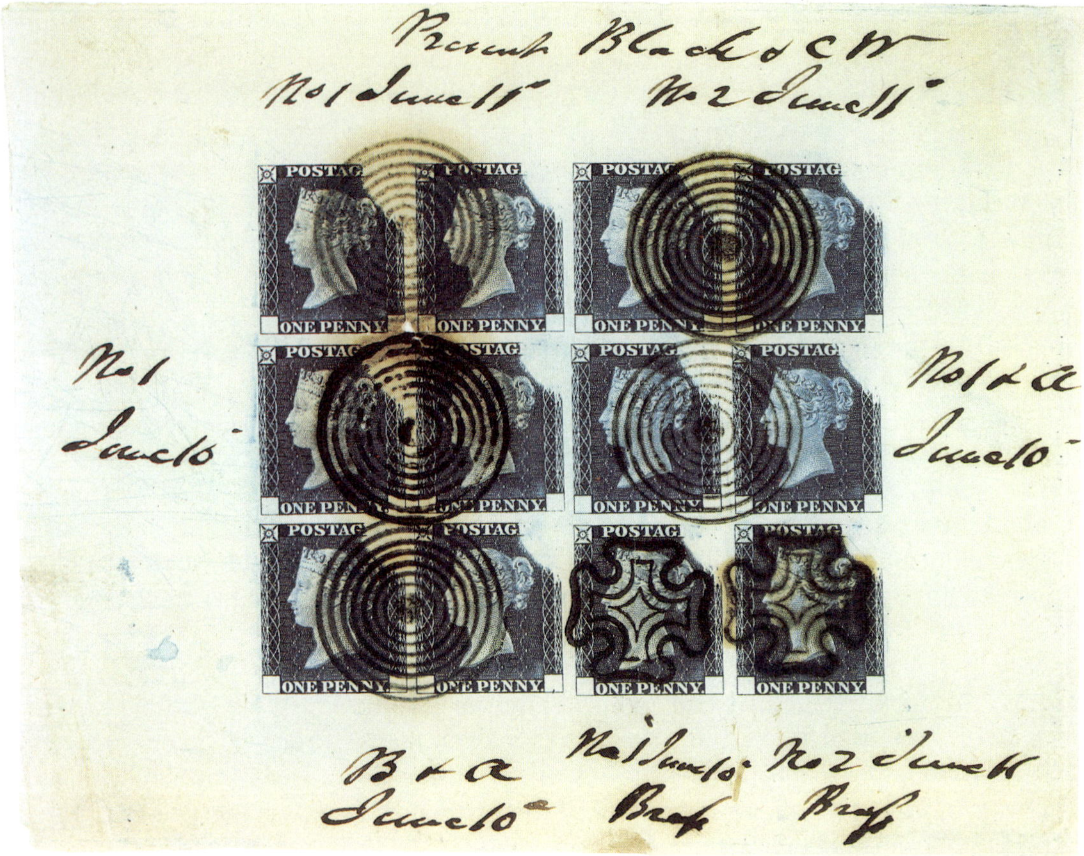

38 A complete sheet of the 'Rainbow' Trials stamps in blue cancelled with a range of experimental black inks. *NPM.*

By 1st September Perkins Bacon had succeeded in concocting new red and blue printing inks which when tested by Professor Phillips were found to be destroyed by any of the chemicals etc which took out the cancelling ink. In the National Postal Museum can be seen two 'Rainbow' Trial sheets printed in the selected alternative red inks. The sheets, after each stamp had been obliterated with the Maltese Cross in black printers ink, were severed and different cleaning agents used in an attempt to remove the cancellations. The sheets were then reconstructed and details of the cleaning agents annotated by Rowland Hill in the margin [illus. 39].

Legend to illustration 39 opposite.

In the accompanying report, dated 17th September 1840, Rowland Hill recommended No. 16 as the colour and ink with which to print the stamps.
The notes in pencil are in Rowland Hill's handwriting; and the agent used in an attempt to remove the obliteration is also noted with each stamp, which has been replaced in its position in the trial sheet of 12.

They are as follows:

No. 9

1 Naphtha and oil of lime
2 Ether and brush
3 Bread and spirits of wine
4 Bread and ether
5 Essential oil
6 Fixed oil
7 Ether
8 Spirits-alum and stream of water
9 Turpentine
10 Soap and water
11 Soap and brush and stream of water

No. 16

1 Naphtha, brush and oil of lime
2 Soap and water and brush
3 Bread after spirits
4 Bread after ether
5 Essential oil
6 Fixed oil
7 Ether
8 Alum, spirits and stream of water
9 Turpentine
10 Soap and water
11 Soap and water
12 Essential oil and bread

39 Two severed sheets of 'Rainbow' Trials stamps printed in alternative experimental red inks *numbers 9 and 16* and used for cancellation removal trials. *NPM.*

But at the end of his report of 17th September to the Chancellor of the Exchequer, Rowland Hill showed that he still had some doubts. *'The arrangement now proposed,'* he wrote, *is, I believe, ...in the present state of chemical knowledge......absolutely secure, but I cannot forget that the red obliterating ink adopted by the Post Office was once considered safe.'*

His apprehensions were soon confirmed. On 7th October he wrote in his diary that *'a Mr. Watson has succeeded in removing the black obliteration from the present black ink stamps. The removal is quite perfect'* – and with practice it could be done in a minute. It could also be done on the (Twopence) stamps printed in the new blue ink. However Watson's method was not so successful with trial stamps printed in the selected red ink. It took a further month's intensive work to produce a modified black cancelling ink which could not be removed without destroying the printing of the stamp itself, whether in red or blue. The black cancelling ink was tried experimentally for a few days at the end of August on letters going through the London District Post.

40 'Rainbow' Trials stamps printed in the new recommended red-brown and blue inks with black experimental cancellations. *NPM.*

This was to prove the solution. On Hill's recommendation (in a second Report date 18th November) the Chancellor agreed that the postage stamps should as soon as practicable be printed with the new inks, the One Penny in red. As for the Twopence there would be no change in colour but a new blue ink would be used [illus. 40]. To assist in distinguishing the old and new printings of the Twopence it was decided to insert horizontal white lines above and below the Queen's portrait.

Hill also recommended his new formula black ink for use with the Maltese Cross handstamps. Though perhaps not perfect it would offer *'superior security under ordinary circumstances'* especially once the supply of the 1840 black stamps had been exhausted. He also strongly advised that future supplies of the cancelling ink should be mixed and provided from London, not left to be mixed by inexperienced staff in country Post Offices.

The New Embossed Stamp Covers

Since 1694 the Stamp Office (of the Inland Revenue) had been using embossing as a secure method of producing various tax stamps, particularly those used on legal documents and licences, such as Game Certificates and Stage Carriage Licences.

A number of the entrants for the Treasury competition of 1839 such as Siever [illus. 41] therefore proposed embossed 'stamps.' Some, such as Charles Whiting, elaborated still further by combining embossing with single or even multi-colour

41 An embossed Treasury Competition essay submitted in 1839 by R. W. Siever. *NPM.*

printing. This method of printing-cum-embossing (the whole was done at one operation in a special press) had been invented earlier by Sir William Congreve and elaborated by Whiting who had married Congreve's widow.

It was this process which Rowland Hill proposed to use for impressing (postage) stamps upon paper of any kind (envelopes, letter sheets etc) brought in by members of the public – one of the alternative methods of the prepayment of postage he had advocated in his 1837 pamphlet.

For the adhesive stamps Hill considered that a combination of an engraved portrait design with watermarked paper would afford ample security against forgery. But in the case of stationery presented by the public there could be no question of a security watermark; it was thus all the more important that the stamp itself should be exceedingly difficult to imitate. Hill therefore recommended (to the Chancellor of The Exchequer on 6th December 1839) that the stamp to be used on 'paper' submitted by members of the public should be similar to Whiting's essay *'but with an embossed head of the Queen in the centre struck from a die to be engraved by Mr. (William) Wyon.'*

At first things went along speedily. The die was commissioned on 11th December from Wyon who started engraving a smaller version of the head he had produced for the City medal of 1838. By 25th January 1840, Wyon and Whiting had together completed a composite die in which the head (in colourless relief) was surrounded by two engine-turned bands, the outer of which was inscribed: 'POSTAGE 1D: HALF OZ' [illus. 42].

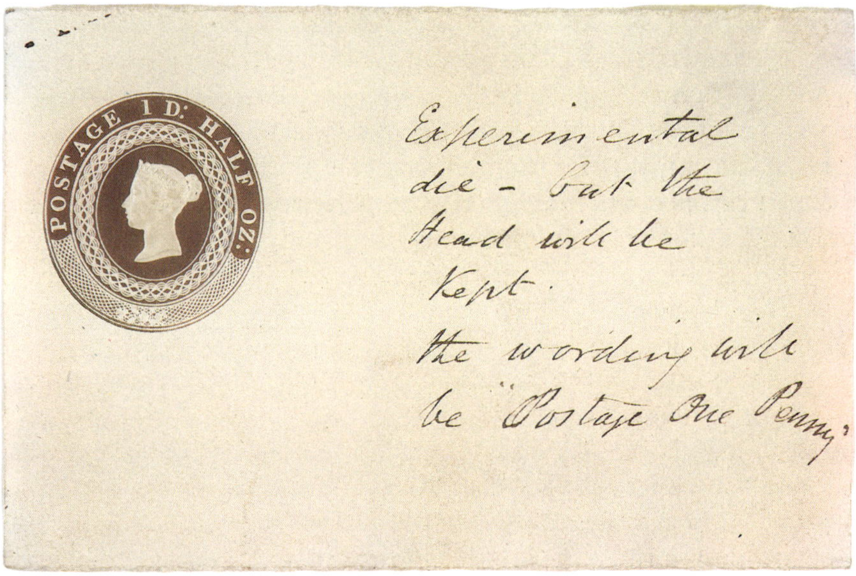

42 A proof *dating from about 25th January 1840* of the embossed stationery die with head by William Wyon and frame etc by Charles Whiting; annotated by Rowland Hill. *NPM.*

By February the wording (as in the adhesive stamps) had been changed to POSTAGE ONE PENNY.' But thereafter the progress of the work slowed down considerably mainly, in Rowland Hill's opinion, as a result of Whiting's 'blundering'. The vital date (1st May) on which the other forms of prepayment were introduced was reached and passed, before the dies were finished; during June there were frustrating delays in preparing the special presses in which the dies were to be used at the Stamp Office.

It is quite possible that the obvious failure of the Mulready covers may have suggested to Hill as early as mid-May that Wyon's embossed dies might come in very usefully to produce new and more acceptable covers. The proposal to offer the facility to the public of having stamps impressed on paper of any description which they might send to the Stamp Office was not formally abandoned, because the Treasury feared forgery, until October 1840. (Stamping-to-order facilities were eventually made available to the public on 8th October 1855.) *'I am sorry,'* Hill wrote in his diary, *'to give up Wyon's stamp for it is a beautiful thing.'*

In fact the Wyon embossed die was not discarded. Sometime during the following month, Hill must have decided that this die could be used instead for the new envelopes which were going to replace the Mulready covers. He must also have succeeded in convincing Baring that there was no real risk of forgery of even an embossed die if it was struck exclusively on Government-issue stationery which was made from security paper incorporating coloured silk threads running diagonally through the paper. Thereafter, over a period of several months, work was directed to perfecting the dies and perfecting and installing the necessary specialised embossing machinery.

A modified version of Wyon's die was finally completed and registered for use on 20th January 1841. The measure of its success with both the Treasury and the Public lies in its continued use right through to the end of the reign.

The New Order

The complete replacement of all the stamps and covers first issued in May 1840 took a surprisingly long time.

The first step was to test the new formula red and blue inks under practical working conditions. Early in December 1840, at Rowland Hill's request, Messrs. Perkins Bacon printed (using a normal plate (No. 8) and the watermarked paper currently in use for the Penny Blacks) four sheets each in the selected red and (two alternative) blue colours. The trial proved successful and the way was clear to print and issue the new, secure, stamps.

Anticipating the colour change, the printing of the One Penny stamps in black had been restricted after August 1840 to just enough copies to meet the day-to-day needs of the Post Office. On 30th December the colour was changed to the selected red and printing in red continued until 20th January 1841. On that date Hill was told that the stock of One Penny stamps in black was almost exhausted, but that the red stamps could not yet be issued because supplies of the new black cancelling ink were not ready. He immediately ordered a provisional final printing of some 10,000 sheets in black, the last of these being printed on 3rd February.

The new red stamps were put on sale on 10th February and at the same time all Post Offices were instructed that *'in future all Postage Stamps are to be obliterated* [cancelled] *with Black Composition* [ink]......' supplies of which were being distributed to them.

Unfortunately the new Twopence stamps (with the white lines added) were not ready at the same time. Printing only started on 27th February and, allowing time for sufficient stocks to be built up, the new stamps were issued about mid-March [illus. 43].

43 The 1841 Two Pence *Plate 3* stamp with white lines above and below the head. *NPM.*

The instructions on changing the colour of the cancelling ink were faithfully observed by all but a very few offices. At these one finds that the red ink continued in use for a few weeks; examples of this irregular usage on either of the 1841 stamps are understandably rare [illus. 44 overleaf].

The 1841-type Penny Red and Twopence Blue stamps continued in use with few alterations – introduction of perforation and a change to letters in all four corners – until 1879-80 when they were replaced by surface-printed (letterpress) stamps manufactured by Thomas De La Rue and Co.

The new stamped stationery to replace Mr. Mulready's discredited covers came out in dribs and drabs. The first replacement, an envelope struck in pale carmine rose with the One Penny version of Wyon's embossed die, was issued late in January 1841 and the corresponding Mulready One Penny envelope withdrawn. The Twopence envelope, with a similar embossed stamp in pale blue, was put on sale in April that same year. Both envelopes [illus. 45 and 46] were printed on the same Dickinson 'security' paper (incorporating silk threads) as had been used for the Mulready covers. These early stamped envelopes were sold by the Post Office unfolded and ungummed, though many stationers supplied them folded etc for a small premium.

The embossed One Penny letter sheet was not issued until May 1844 when the corresponding Mulready letter sheet was withdrawn. The Twopence Mulready letter sheet was never replaced. The new embossed postal stationery was so successful that it continued to be used, virtually unaltered, until the end of the reign.

44 The 1841 One Penny red cancelled *contrary to regulations* with a *red* Maltese Cross. *NPM.*

45-46 The new One Penny and Two Pence embossed pre-paid envelopes. *NPM.*

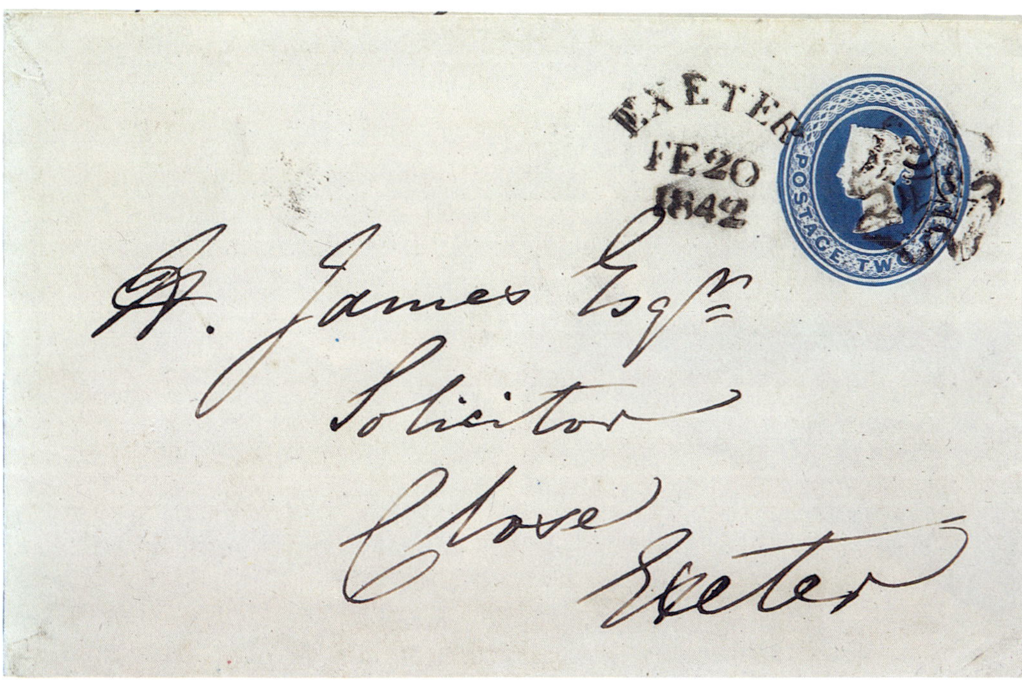

Short Chronology

1837	January		Rowland Hill publishes, privately his pamphlet on 'Post Office Reform......'
	February	14th	R. Hill proposes, in evidence to the Duncannon Commission on the Post Office, the use of adhesive stamped labels as a method of prepayment of postage.
	November		Parliamentary Select Committee on Postage begins work.
1838	February		Formation of the Mercantile Committee *of the City of London* which organised the propaganda for Uniform Postage, until July 1839.
	February	8th	James Chalmers produced the world's first stamp essays, *which he called 'slips.'*
	August	13th	Parliamentary Select Committee on Postage reports in favour of reform.
1839	July	18-29th	Postage Bill passes all stages in House of Commons.
	August	17th	Postage Act receives Royal Assent and becomes law.
	September	6th	Treasury Minute, published in *The Times,* invites proposals from the public as to methods for the prepayment of postage and offers prizes *Treasury Competition.*
	September	7th	R. Hill starts his diary. *Post Office Journal.*
	September	16th	R. Hill appointed to the Treasury.
	October	8th	Henry Cole begins work as R. Hill's assistant.
	October	15th	Close of Treasury Competition.
	November	2nd	R. Hill submits his plan for implementing Uniform Postage to the Chancellor of the Exchequer, Sir F. Baring.
	December	5th	Introduction of Uniform Fourpenny Postage.
	December	6th	Report of R. Hill to the Chancellor of the Exchequer on the Proposed Franking System.
	December	11th	Chancellor of the Exchequer authorises Hill to commence preparation of stamps etc. W. Wyon commissioned to engrave die of the Queen's head.
	December	16th	W. Mulready completes his stationery design.
	December	26th	Treasury authority given for the preparation of the four different types of 'stamps.'
	December	31st	Perkins Bacon & Co. ordered to prepare a die for the postage stamp.

1840	January		Heath starts engraving of first stamp die.
	January	6th	J. Thompson commissioned to engrave Mulready die.
	January	10th	Introduction of Uniform Penny Postage.
	January	15-16th	First stamp die completed *and rejected*, second stamp die started.
	January	16th	Houses of Parliament prepaid stationery issued.
	January	25th	Wyon's embossed die *head only* completed.
	January	31st	Edwin Hill appointed Superintendant of Stamps at the Stamping Office, Somerset House.
	February	20th	Second *accepted* stamp die, head completed.
	March	31st	Master die of Penny completed.
	April	1st	Mulready die completed.
	April	2nd	First proof sheet of the One Penny stamp printed and approved by Baring.
	April	3rd	Mulready proofs shown to the Queen.
	April	15th	Printing of Mulready covers started.
	April	16th	Printing of One Penny Stamps started.
	May	1st	One Penny stamps and Mulready covers put on sale.
	May	2nd	Printing of Two Pence stamps started.
	May	6th	Stamps and Mulready stationery becomes valid for postage.
	May	8th	Two Pence stamps put on sale in London.
	August	*end*	Experimental use in black of Maltese Cross cancel at London.
	September	17th	R. Hill's first report on the Obliteration of Postage Stamps.
	November	18th	R. Hill's second report on the Obliteration of Postage Stamps.
	December	19th	New Red and Blue colours agreed for 1d and 2d stamps.
	December	30th	Printing of One Penny red stamps started.
1841	January	21st	Provisional final printing of One Penny black stamps *to 3rd February.*
	January	*late*	One Penny pink embossed envelopes put on sale.
	February	10th	One Penny red stamps put on sale.
	February	27th	Printing of new Two Pence stamps started.
	March	*mid*	Two Pence blue stamps *with white lines* put on sale.
	April		Two Pence blue embossed envelope put on sale.
1844	May		One Penny embossed letter sheet put on sale.

Personalities of the Penny Black Story

Bacon *Joshua Butters* -1863.

Printer: married the daughter of Jacob Perkins; Joined his father-in-law's firm in 1821, and by 1839 was the effective head of Perkins, Bacon & Petch who printed British postage stamps 1840-79.

Baring *Sir Francis* 1796-1866.

MP for Portsmouth 1826-1865; Chancellor of the Exchequer August 1839 to September 1841; First Lord of the Admiralty 1849-52; 1st Baron Northbrook 1866.

Chalmers *James* 1782-1853.

Bookseller, binder and printer at Castle Street, Dundee; active as a critic of the postal system during the 1830s; originator of the first printed postage stamp essays dated 10th February 1838.

Cole *Sir Henry* 1808-1882.

Public Records Commission and Office 1823-38; Secretary of the Mercantile Committee 1838-39; Assistant to Rowland Hill at the Treasury 1840-42; artist, etcher and book illustrator, exhibited at the Royal Academy; Member and Chairman 1851-52 of the *Royal* Society of Arts; Member of the Executive Committee of the Great Exhibition 1851; Part-founder of the Albert Hall 1862 and the Royal College of Music and of the Victoria and Albert Museum of which he was first secretary *Director* 1859-73; KCB 1875.

Corbould *Henry* 1787-1844.

Pupil at the Royal Academy Schools; exhibited at the RA from 1807; book illustrator; drew the Elgin Marbles etc for the British Museum portfolios.

Doyle *John* 1797-1868.

Irish painter and caricaturist; exhibited at the RA; best known for a long series of caricatures of famous men 1829-51. His son Richard Doyle 1824-83 was on the staff of *Punch* from 1843, and was a well-known watercolourist and book illustrator.

Heath *Charles* 1785-1848.

Engraver; Fellow of the Society of British Artists; producer of several series of books including 'Heath's Book of Beauty.'

Hill *Edwin* 1793-1876.

Brother of Sir R. Hill; inventor and writer on currency matters; Superintendent of Letter Stamps at the Inland Revenue from 1840. Retired 1872.

Hill *Pearson.*

Son of Sir R. Hill; served in the Post Office and is best remembered as the inventor of the Parallel Motion cancelling machine.

Hill *Sir Rowland* FRS, DCL 1795-1879.

Born at Kidderminster; school teacher from 1807; wrote on liberal Educational Reform 1822; inventor in the fields of transport and printing; Secretary of the South Australian Colonisation Commission 1835-39; concerned with postal reform from 1826 onwards; appointed to the Treasury to implement his Uniform Postage plan 1839-42; Railway Director 1842-46; Secretary to the PMG 1846-54; Secretary to the 'Post Office' 1854-64; Knighted 1860.

Knight *Charles* 1791-1873.

Author and publisher; 1830: Superintendent of publications of the Society for the Diffusion of Useful Knowledge; published the Penny Magazine and the *Quarterly Journal of Education.*

Leech *John* 1817-1864.

Trained as a doctor at Barts but turned to illustrating; his caricature of Mulready's cover made his reputation; joined the staff of *Punch* in August 1841 until 1864, during which period he produced 3,000 drawings; friend of Ruskin, Thackerary and W. P. Frith.

Maberley *Lt. Col. William Leader* 1798-1885.

A serving soldier until 1834; Secretary of the Post Office 1836-1854.

Mulready *William* RA 1786-1863.

Genre painter and book illustrator; student at the Royal Academy Schools 1800-; exhibited at the RA from 1804.

Perkins *Jacob* 1766-1849.

A native of Philadelphia; a printer and inventor who revived, in the USA, the method of printing from engraved steel plates and applied it to the security printing of bank-notes; he came to England in 1819 and formed the firm of Perkins Bacon in 1829.

Thompson *John.*

Engraver; who, apart from the 'Mulready' die, engraved the Britannia on the Penny coin and parts of the pre-1939 £5 note.

Wyon *William* RA 1795-1851.

Chief Engraver at the Royal Mint 1826-51; received the Gold Medal of the Royal Society of Arts in 1813 and was first engraver to receive a medal from the Royal Academy 1838; entered the Royal Mint in 1816.

The Reginald M. Phillips Collection, a Note

The National Postal Museum was opened in 1965 to provide a permanent home for the unique collection of nineteenth century British postage stamps which had just been presented to the Post Office – in trust for the nation – by the late Reginald M. Phillips CBE. It was also to house the Post Office's own stamp archives which included the surviving proof sheets of the 1840 and 1841 issues.

The Phillips Collection is one of the two greatest collections ever formed of British postage stamps up to the end of Queen Victoria's reign; the other being that formed by King George V and now part of the Royal Collection at Buckingham Palace.

Mr. Phillips' particular interest lay in the story of the origin, design and production of the world's first adhesive postage stamps – the 1d black and 2d blue of May 1840 – and that section of his collection contains a remarkable array of unique items of outstanding philatelic importance. Many of these are illustrated in this book. But, additionally, the Phillips Collection contains superb mint and used examples of the stamps (including some outstanding multiples) as well as a wealth of fine covers and all the important varieties.

Although the items from the collection of H.M. The Queen and the Cole Bequest are not on public view, the whole of the Phillips Collection is permanently on display in the National Postal Museum, which is situated in the London Chief (Post) Office building in King Edward Street, very close to St. Pauls Underground Station.
The National Postal Museum is open Mondays to Fridays (except Bank Holidays) from 10am to 4.30pm. Entrance is free.

Suggestions for Further Reading

The British Postage Stamp in the Nineteenth Century
by Robson Lowe.
The National Postal Museum, London 1969. *2nd Edition* 1979.

Sir Rowland Hill
by J. V. Farrugia.
The National Postal Museum, London 1979.

Postage Stamps of Great Britain
Part 1
The Imperforate Line-Engraved Issues
by J. B. Seymour and C. Gardiner-Hill.
Royal Philatelic Society, 1967.

British Postal Stationery
by Dr. A. K. Huggins.
Great Britain Philatelic Society. 2nd Edition 1972.

The Mulready Envelope and its Caricatures
by Major J. B. Evans.
reprinted from the 1891 *Edition. Stanley Gibbons Limited* 1970.

Acknowledgements

Illustrations have been reproduced
by courtesy of

H.M. The Queen

Cole Bequest, Victoria & Albert Museum

Public Record Office

John Guthrie Esq.